SAILING
Between the
STARS

musings on the mysteries of faith

STEVEN JAMES

Revell
Grand Rapids, Michigan

Published by Fleming H. Revell
a division of Baker Publishing Group
P.O. Box 6287, Grand Rapids, MI 49516-6287
www.revellbooks.com

Printed in the United States of America

Library of Congress Cataloging-in-Publication Data
James, Steven, 1969-
   Sailing between the stars : musings on the mysteries of faith / Steven James.
         p.   cm.
   Includes bibliographical references.
   ISBN 10: 0-8007-3164-6 (pbk.)
   ISBN 978-0-8007-3164-9 (pbk.)
   1. Spirituality. 2.Mystery. 3. Christianity. 4. James, Steven, 1969- I. Title.
BV4501.3.J362 2006
242—dc22   2006014942

to the friend who taught me
"you do not become a poet,
a poet becomes you."

it is true
about
so many things.

If we submit everything to reason our religion will be left with nothing mysterious or supernatural.

Blaise Pascal, seventeenth-century philosopher
and mathematician

The most beautiful thing we can experience is the mysterious.

Albert Einstein, physicist and genius

contents

acknowledgments

Thanks to Liesl, Esther, Pam, and Sonya for reading through earlier drafts of this book and for offering your helpful comments and suggestions. I am indebted to you for your ideas and thankful to you for your honesty. Jayne, thanks for letting me share the story of the little queen. Thanks to Pamela for your encouragement and to Kristin, Jen, Suzie, Aaron, and the rest of the great folks at Baker Publishing Group for your trust, enthusiasm, and vision. The wind is picking up. Keep raising your sails higher.

in the company of fools

When one of my daughters (no, I'm not telling you which one) was six months old, she would beat herself in the face with anything we stuck in the crib with her. Including the hamster. When she turned eighteen months old, she would dig through the trash cans, pull out used Q-tips, and chew on them. And then when she turned three years old, she would take all her clothes off whenever we had company over and run throughout the house screaming, "I'm naked! I'm naked!" I remember thinking, *Great. I've managed to raise a three-year-old suicidal Q-tip–eating stripper.*

She was five when my brother got married. After the wedding, she sat next to her new aunt and started licking her arm.

"Stop that!" I told her.

"I'm kissing her the grown-up way," my daughter said innocently.

"You mean with your tongue?"

"Mm-hmm."

My new sister-in-law just sat on the couch staring at me as her niece licked her arm. I decided not to bring up the Q-tip eating and the stripping.

Over the years I've taken note of stupid signs I've seen around the country. On the door of a grocery store I once saw a sign that said, "Push. Do Not Enter." A friend of mine told me he saw a sign in West Virginia that read, "Free kittens for sale." In Virginia I saw a sign with lights around it near a construction site. The sign read, "Construction workers present when flashing." I drove by thinking, *That's the last thing I wanna see.* Think about it. I bet you'll agree.

Humans are peculiar. We do stupid, inexplicable things. At every mall in America you'll find teenage girls wearing shorts with words written on the butt. I saw a girl with the word *Kentucky* written on the seat of her pants. I wondered if it was a good thing or a bad thing to have the name of your state written on someone's butt. Does it mean she's a fan? Anti-fan? I saw a girl with *cute* written on her shorts. I sat there trying to figure out just what part of her anatomy that was supposed to be referring to. I saw this other girl with *all-star* written on her butt. I don't even wanna know what that means.

Humans are indeed an odd, entertaining, bewildering breed full of mishaps and blunders. In this world of baffling people, it's not always clear who's on your side and who isn't. I've found you need to be careful who you trust. I have a personal policy to avoid guys who name their trucks Alice, grown men who wear Velcro shoes, and people who use camouflage flashlights. But that's just me. You can come up with your own criteria.

Yet as bizarre and screwed up as we are, beauty is threaded through our stories. Glory, dignity, and grace bubble up from our souls. We can tell we're from here but don't belong here. We're meant for more than this. We are dust and bones and blood and dreams, skin-covered spirits with hungry souls. We are Hitler and Gandhi; Genghis Khan and Martin Luther King Jr. We are nurses and terrorists, lovers and liars, suicide bombers and little grinning children with milk mustaches.

Sometimes we kiss like grown-ups, and sometimes we sell free kittens.

sailing between the stars

My sixth-grade daughter was studying for a spelling bee, and one of the advanced words was *agathokakological*. It took us awhile to track down the definition: "consisting of both good and evil." What a fabulous word: *agathokakological*. We humans have agathokakological hearts, motives, dreams, passions. The next day I told my youngest daughter to inform her first-grade teacher that we are an agathokakological breed. I wish I could have seen the teacher's expression when Eden told her that.

Chesterton called us "broken gods." Pascal called us "fallen princes." Philosophers have long wondered how we fit into this world, somewhere between the apes and the angels. To make us into one or the other is to deny the full reality of who we are, because we have both animal instincts and divine desires. Pascal (a philosopher), wrote, "Man must not think that he is on a level either with the brutes or with the angels, nor must he be ignorant of both sides of his nature; but he must know both."[1] Rumi (a mystic poet), wrote, "Half of him is angelic and half animal. . . . The angel is free because of his knowledge, the beast because of his ignorance. Between the two remains the son of man to struggle."[2] A friend of mine told me that we are each Cinderella in the moment of transformation—half dressed in ashes and rags, half clothed in a royal gown ready to meet the prince.

Agathokakological.

We're from below and from above, bestial and celestial, children of the earth and offspring of the stars. We are an odd race capable of both martyrdom and murder, poetry and rape, worship and abortion. And Christianity explains why: we are both the Spirit-breathed children of God and the expelled rebels of the kingdom. In the ways that matter most, we're all from the Garden of Eden. We've all listened to the snake. Yet we're also children of the Father. We are far worse than we would ever on our own admit and loved by God more deeply than we would ever dare to dream. We are both worthless and priceless, terrorists and saints, lost and homeward bound.

> the wrinkles of a child's toes
> and the wrinkles on a father's brow
> tell me who i really am.
> > both more and less
> > human than i'd ever
> > hoped to be.

∽

Everywhere you look in Christianity, you see mysteries piled upon mysteries.

Here, death is the beginning of life, foolishness is the pathway to wisdom, the meek conquer the strong, a lamb tramples a snake, and the almighty Creator of the galaxies has a belly button. The foundation of this faith is paradox, not common sense—because logic can only take you as far as the confines of language and reason, but paradox can lead you all the way to the truth.

This is the story that bookends the ages. One day the garden with the dragon who infects souls will be transformed into the garden where the Dove reigns forever. Here is a tale bigger than life but just the right size to fit in your heart.

In the crazy world of Christianity, those who think themselves wise are really fools in disguise, while those who know they're fools become our greatest prophets and teachers. Those who are the most aware of their sins are our greatest saints, while those who think they're not really all that bad (at least compared to most people) are the greatest sinners. Those who think they're humble are proud, but those who know they're proud are humble. Those who believe themselves to be free are the most enchained; those who see their chains are finally free.

sailing between the stars

As long as I think I can see, I'm blind. And only when I'm brave enough to admit that I'm beyond all hope does hope come crashing in and cleanse my heart.

We're told to set our eyes on what we cannot see, accept a peace that's beyond understanding, know a love that surpasses knowledge, and cling to the certainty of what we cannot prove. One day when my mind was spinning with all these paradoxes of faith, I prayed this prayer:

> o elegant mystery,
> creator of time,
> revealer of history,
> tune of the chime,
> echo and swirl and curl through
> my mind.
>> here i am waiting to be found
>> and to find.
> seeker and shepherd,
> blossom of laws,
> lion of conquest sharpen your claws,
> here i am waiting,
> a child of your light;
> no more debating
> with my soul in the night.
> circle and stir and renew my soul
> o elegant mystery
>> splinter me whole.

To be splintered into wholeness is the goal of the Jesus-focused life.

∽

I think one of the most attractive and most neglected aspects of Christian spirituality is the idea that Jesus is a mystery. For example, St. Paul begged his fellow believers to pray for him so that he and his ministry team might have more opportunities to "proclaim the mystery of Christ" (Colossians 4:3 NIV). Not too many pastors talk like that today. Rather than proclaim the mystery of Christ, they explain the truth about God. This is much safer territory. All too often, modern Christianity locks mystery outside in the yard while we gather together to talk about truth in the living room.

It's an odd approach when you look at the New Testament's emphasis on Jesus as both truth and mystery. And it's even more perplexing when you look at how hungry the emerging postmodern world is for mystery, wonder, and transcendence. Rather than sharing the paradoxes of Christianity with our neopagan neighbors, we're busy trying to make Jesus seem reasonable, sensible, and practical. But he's not. He's radical, paradoxical, and absurd.

And that's one of the reasons he's so attractive to me.

That's one of the reasons I believe.

An easily definable little plaything of a God wouldn't be all that interesting, but a God big enough to speak love into time is endlessly intriguing.

It isn't that our faith is ridiculous; it's just that it appears so foolish to all who aren't fools. How could we hang our hat on so many paradoxical doctrines at the same time? Well, because the prism of paradox is the place God has chosen to shine his light. And because of that, it can't help but glow in so many different colors at once.

Christianity promises a cross to carry, along with a Lord who offers to tote our burdens. Christianity promises comfort from God and persecution from the world, love and hatred, life and death, joy and suffering in the same breath, as well as a strange kind of freedom that looks an awful lot like being in slavery to God. Paul described the lives of believers like this: "We are hard pressed on every side, but not crushed; perplexed, but not in despair; persecuted, but not abandoned; struck down, but not destroyed. We always carry around in our body the death of Jesus, so that the life of Jesus may also be revealed in our body" (2 Corinthians 4:8–10 NIV).

I read stuff like that and I think, *Huh? How does all that work?* A few chapters later Paul continues, "We are honest, but they call us impostors. We are well known, but we are treated as unknown. We live close to death, but here we are, still alive. We have been beaten within an inch of our lives. Our hearts ache, but we always have joy. We are poor, but we give spiritual riches to others. We own nothing, and yet we have everything" (2 Corinthians 6:8–10).

Agathokakological.

And when it comes to the thorny issues of evil, pain, and suffering, we're not told to just put up with them or deal with them the best we can, because that would make too much sense. Instead, believers are commanded to delight in our weaknesses, trust in God through our pain, and then embrace our sufferings as the most intimate way of identifying with the death of Jesus.

The very things the Western world embraces with both arms—materialism, ambition, individualism, and self-love—are exact opposites of biblical Christianity, in which you can't serve both God and materialism, greed is the same as idolatry, the needs of the community trump the desires of the individual, and self-love is the pathway to certain destruction, not to enlightenment.

My daughter (the one who eats Q-tips and kisses like a grown-up) likes to pray, "God, I love you so, so, so, so, so much!" because she's not only my child—confused and agathokakological and a little bit weird—but his daughter too, tugging on the pants leg of the divine. "I can't wait until I die," she told me once, "because then I get to be with Jesus! And I'm gonna have a giant tree house in heaven, and Furnelia [her stuffed unicorn] will be real, and she'll be able to talk, and I'll even let you visit me, Daddy!" At first I was a little disturbed by my little girl's death wish, but then I remembered that St. Paul, perhaps the world's greatest theologian, said almost exactly the same thing (see Philippians 1:21–24). Here, in the faith of Jesus, we learn our deepest spiritual truths from pint-sized strippers.

Jesus taught that only those who release their grip on this life will receive the fullness of new life he offers. Those who play it safe lose out, while those who risk all are given a place in the kingdom.

What kind of strange religion is this with paradoxes at every corner and the ludicrous idea that every square inch of the universe has been saturated with bloody love?

The more I think about these things and the more I explore the reality of Jesus, the more I feel like a child pulling on the hem of a mystery. But instead of seeing my faith unravel, I see it grow stronger and more intact, somehow more complex and simpler at the same time.

Every once in a while a skeptic of Christianity will point out these paradoxes as a way of trying to attack the foundations of our faith. But followers of Jesus are already aware of them. We're the first to admit that our God isn't logical, our religion isn't reasonable, and our Savior isn't realistic. Here is our message: we're fools for God; come join us under the big top.

seeing with God-shaped eyes

My daughters and I have this bedtime routine where I ask them questions about the Bible and purposely get everything mixed up. It goes something like this: "Okay, Eden, you're next. When Jesus was born, did his mother lay him (a) in a dinosaur's mouth, (b) in a hot dog bun, or (c) in a manger?"

Eden, who is six, shouts, "A!"

And I act completely shocked by her answer. "No! She didn't put the baby Jesus in a dinosaur's mouth!"

Her eyes light up. "B!"

I tickle her relentlessly. "Mary didn't stick him in *a hot dog bun*!"

"C! C! C!" she squeals. Then it's her sister's turn. You get the picture.

So we were doing this one night with the Parable of the Guys Sorting the Fish (see Matthew 13:47–51) and after doing the goof-off routine, I decided to end on a more serious note. "Now," I said, "in this story, the fisherman separates the good fish from the bad fish. Which fish represent the believers?"

"The bad fish!" says Ariel, who is ten and hasn't figured out I've turned the corner and am now being serious.

"Um, no."

"Um, the good fish?" says Eden.

"Right!"

Then Trinity, who is eleven, says, "I have a question. If the fisherman took the good fish to eat and the bad ones he threw back into the water, which one would I want to be?"

Hmm.

"Um, I never thought of that." And then, trying to retain my reputation as the resident Bible scholar in our house, I decided to shift the subject, just like all good teachers do when they're stumped. "Are you telling me you want to be a bad fish?"

"I don't want to be eaten. If God keeps the good fish as his pets, then I want to be a good fish."

"Okay," I said. "He does. You can be his pet."

"Good. 'Cause I don't wanna be eaten."

I have no idea if God would agree with my interpretation that he makes believers his heavenly pets. Probably not, but it seemed like the right thing to say at the time. At least it was better than teaching my kids that we all get eaten in heaven.

I love that Jesus told his followers they couldn't enter his kingdom unless they became more like kids. Of course I don't think he's talking about the whining, biting, fussing, pouting, picking-on-the-girl-with-braces aspects of childhood but about the stuff like curiosity, trust, charity, unbridled enthusiasm, unfaltering faith, and stark honesty. Kids love to go to parties, just like God; they love to play pretend, just like Jesus; and so they are uniquely qualified to point out the mystery and marvel that chase each other through everyday life.

God doesn't want us to admire him like a statue but to love him like a daddy. As Frederick Buechner wrote, "When Jesus is asked who is the greatest in the kingdom of Heaven, he reaches into the crowd and pulls out a child with a cheek full of bubble gum and eyes full of whatever a child's eyes are full of and says unless you can become like that, don't bother to ask."[1]

A few weeks ago Eden started turning to an empty corner of the room and shouting with outstretched arms, "I love you, Daddy!"

"Um, I'm over here," I told her.

"I was talking to God," she replied.

∽

I think if I were to create a religion from scratch, it wouldn't look a whole lot like Christianity. It would be full of hard work and equal rewards and fair play. It'd be practical and sensible and have just the right amount of positive reinforcement and clever, comforting psychobabble. It wouldn't include so much mystery and sacrifice, just lots of affirmations so people could feel good about themselves.

It wouldn't exclude anyone from heaven; instead I'd make the road to life easy and the road to destruction hard. I'd tell people to be true to themselves and follow their hearts and pursue their dreams. After all, we only go around once and *carpe diem* and you deserve a break today and various other catchy spiritual dictums. It would be a nice, helpful, cream-filled religion that's low in saturated fats and cholesterol. That's the kind of religion I'd make up.

But it's not the kind I need.

I need a truth as deep as the night and a hope as rich as the dawn. I need Jesus.[2]

Imagination dwells at the heart of Christianity. It's a worldview of wonder. Actually, it's not technically a worldview at all because it's not a way of viewing the world but a different way of living upon this world altogether. It's an inner transformation of all the important aspects of being human—passions, goals, dreams, desires, loves, priorities, wonderments. And it's packed full of paradox . . . which makes many believers today uncomfortable.

The early Christian church wasn't nearly as wary of mystery as we are today. In fact, I'd say they tended to celebrate it rather than shy away from it. "I want you woven into a tapestry of love," wrote St. Paul, "in touch with everything there is to know of God. Then you will have minds confident and at rest, focused on Christ, God's great mystery" (Colossians 2:2 Message). I love that thought—confident and at rest and focused on God's great mystery. I can think of worse ways to spend your life and your eternity.

The Athanasian Creed, one of the four authoritative creeds of the Catholic Church, dives headfirst into the mystery of God. When someone handed me a copy of this creed a few years ago I was shocked (and thrilled) to find paradoxes soaking through nearly every line.

This is what the Catholic faith teaches: we worship one God in the Trinity and the Trinity in unity. Neither confounding the Persons, nor dividing the substance.

For there is one person of the Father, another of the Son, another of the Holy Spirit. But the Father and the Son and the Holy Spirit have one divinity, equal glory, and coeternal majesty.

What the Father is, the Son is, and the Holy Spirit is. The Father is uncreated, the Son is uncreated, and the Holy Spirit is uncreated. The Father is boundless, the Son is boundless, and the Holy Spirit is boundless. The Father is eternal, the Son is eternal, and the Holy Spirit is eternal. Nevertheless, there are not three eternal beings, but one eternal being. So there are not three uncreated beings, nor three boundless beings, but one uncreated being and one boundless being.

Likewise, the Father is omnipotent, the Son is omnipotent, the Holy Spirit is omnipotent. Yet there are not three omnipotent beings, but one omnipotent being. Thus the Father is God, the Son is God, and the Holy Spirit is God. However, there are not three gods, but one God. The Father is Lord, the Son is Lord, and the Holy Spirit is Lord. However, there are not three lords, but one Lord.

For as we are obliged by Christian truth to acknowledge every Person singly to be God and Lord, so too are we forbidden by the Catholic religion to say that there are three Gods or Lords.

The Father was not made, nor created, nor generated by anyone. The Son is not made, nor created, but begotten by the Father alone. The Holy Spirit is not made, nor created, nor generated, but proceeds from the Father and the Son. There is, then, one Father, not three fathers; one Son, not three sons; one Holy Spirit, not three holy spirits. In this Trinity, there is nothing before or after, nothing greater or less. The entire three Persons are coeternal and coequal with one another.

So that in all things, as has been said above, the Unity is to be worshipped in Trinity and the Trinity in Unity. He, therefore, who wishes to be saved, must believe thus about the Trinity.

Whether or not you agree with (or even understand) all the points in this confession of faith, there's no denying that mystery is held front and center. The mysterious aspects of God aren't diminished or disguised or swept under the rug. They're hung up above the fireplace for everyone to see. If anything, God becomes more indefinable and mysterious than ever.

I love this approach. It keeps God where he should be: within reach of my heart, but not of my mind.

billions upon billions
of moments wrapped up
in billions upon billions
of stars. the edge of space
inhales and expands into
another thought unfolding
in the mind of God.
     and yet, he keeps track of
     all the hairs on my head,
     and the dreams in my heart,
     and the doubts masquerading as loves
     in the ribcage of my dreams.

how radiant the mystery must be
to offer such unblemished love.
no wonder i can't look into his eyes
and live. i would die from
either the glory
     or the terror.
either would be too much for me
to ever breathe again.

The kingdom of God is the kingdom of fools and children looking up into the eyes of an invisible Daddy.

One time Jesus actually prayed this odd prayer: "O Father, Lord of heaven and earth, thank you for hiding the truth from those who think themselves so wise and clever, and for revealing it to the childlike" (Luke 10:21). What a fabulous prayer. Earlier in the verse Luke even emphasizes that Jesus was filled with the Holy Spirit when he said those words. Jesus, filled with the Holy Spirit, actually thanked God for hiding the truth from stuck-up know-it-alls. That is so fantastic.

I've been tempted to pray this prayer about certain people I know, but not in times when I was filled with the Holy Spirit.

Only the childlike believe. Only children can walk through heaven's doors. To enter the Nazarene's kingdom, we need to become less mature, not more mature, because old age is determined not by a hardening of the arteries but by a hardening of the heart. No one is old who sees the world through a child's God-shaped eyes.

souls in the belly of the beasts

my daughter ariel told her hamster that he needed to believe in jesus, and she prayed with him so that he would be able to go to heaven.

"all animals have souls," her older sister, trinity, says.

"how do you know that?" i ask.

"i just know they do. i know horses do. i *know* they do."

and so i tell them that when i was a kid my pet turtle died and i didn't know if he would be in heaven and my dad told me he would, and that in the bible it talks about the lion lying down with the lamb and a rider on a white horse coming at the end of time and it wouldn't say that unless there were animals there, right?

and my daughters nod and agree that animals go to heaven because they have learned to talk to hamsters and have seen the beauty of stallions running in the sun.

Our friends Mark and Nancy had been trying to have a baby for years without any success. It was devastating to them. They asked us to pray for them, and so one night when Trinity was six, she prayed the following two prayers. I hurried up from her bedside as soon as she was done and wrote them down. I couldn't stand the thought of them disappearing into the folds of time. Here they are:

God,

please help Miss Nancy have a baby.

and just in case you get mixed up,

—even though you probably won't,

but just in case you do—

remember not to put the nose in the belly button place

and the belly button in the nose place

and the mouth in the foot place

and the feet in the mouth place.

amen.

and God,

thanks for sending Eden to our family

and looking all over and making sure

we were the right family

and thanks for finding two big sisters

who were just the right big sisters for her.

amen.

Those are two of the most magnificent prayers I've ever heard.

And God did just as Trinity asked. Four months later Jonathan was conceived. He'll be five on December 15 of this year. And thankfully, God remembered not to put the nose in the belly button place and the belly button in the nose place and the mouth in the foot place, and so on. This is one prayer I'm really glad God answered in whole, right down to the last detail.

Theology is our attempt to capture God in the butterfly net of our minds. But, of course, he's too wild for that. In one of the great ironies of faith, the more we try to pin God down, the less spiritual we become.

When we try to comprehend him, to package him up and explain him to the world, we diminish ourselves. After all, no one has ever been moved to tears by reading someone's resume. To really get to know a person, you get together for a cup of coffee or a bratwurst on the back deck. You become friends by sharing your hopes and dreams, your passions and fears, your heartaches and wounds and secret little embarrassing moments, not by studying someone's transcripts, work history, or dental records.

Yet when it comes to getting to know God, for some reason Christians all too often try to break him down into bite-sized pieces that fit neatly into one-page doctrinal statements and three-point sermons. We call it systematic theology, but the problem is, theology isn't systematic. It's narrative. God isn't a subject to be studied; he's a Person to be encountered.

That's why the Bible is the story of God and not the lesson about God. The minute we try to draw lines through the story to explain it all in easy-to-digest morsels, it unravels. You can never experience the full flavor of a story by dissecting it; you experience it only by devouring it with the wide-open mouth of your soul. God isn't an algebra problem to be solved. He is the heartbeat of the universe.

I find that when I honestly explore God's story, I don't often come away with a neat package of spiritual answers. Usually I end up with more questions than ever—but more comfort too. I think those on the road to understanding are the curious souls, the questioning ones, the childlike. But the people with all the answers haven't even laced up their boots to begin the journey.

When Trinity was in kindergarten, I tried to explain to her how God could be everywhere at once. "Well," I said, leaning my arm on her bed, "Daddy is on the floor and he's also on your bed. I'm in two places at once. It's just that God is so big, he's everywhere at once!" There. That was easy. Theology 101.

"How come we can't see him?"

"Well, he's invisible."

"How come he doesn't squish us?"

"Um, because he's a spirit, like air."

She thought about that for a moment. "Do we breathe him in?"

I was just about ready to explain that no, of course not, we don't breathe God in, that's ridiculous, but then I remembered a Bible verse about us living in God, about him being in every breath we take (it's Acts 17:28—I had to look it up later).

"Hmm. Um, well, in a way we do."

"How?"

Now, a parent can only take so many *hows* and *whys*. Sooner or later we come to the point of saying, "I don't know" or, "Because I said so, *that's* why!" And when it comes to God, the goofy question games, explanations, definitions, and creeds all fall short eventually. No matter how much we learn or how spiritual we become, there will always be one more *how?*, one more *why?*

So I sighed, "Well, he's kind of a mystery, honey."

"Oh," she said. And then, "I love Jesus, Daddy."

"Me too."

And then, after another pause, "I like mysteries too."

"Yeah," I said. "So do I."

And then I held her hand for a while as she rolled onto her side to go to sleep. Soon her breathing changed and she grew calmer and stiller in the night. Inhaling God with every breath.

mystery is where i live

To celebrate our tenth anniversary, my wife, Liesl, and I went to Hawaii. Toward the end of our trip as we were driving along the coastline, I noticed a used bookstore. Now, I love books way more than any normal, relatively well-adjusted person should. So when I see a used bookstore, I'm like a Pavlovian dog. I started salivating all over the rental car. "Okay," said Liesl. "We can stop, but only for a few minutes. Now stop drooling."

"Yes, yes, books, books," I said.

As we walked inside, she reminded me how little space we had in our luggage, so I limited myself to just half a dozen books. The bearded and grizzled bookstore owner glanced at the titles. When he saw G. K. Chesterton's *Orthodoxy* in my stack, he said, "This is a good book."

"I've heard that," I said.

And then, before I knew what was happening, we were neck-deep in a conversation about philosophy and culture and spirituality. This guy knew his stuff; I was way out of my league. Finally he said, "You know what I think is wrong with our culture?"

"No. What's that?"

He stared past me thoughtfully. "I have this image in mind that illustrates it—I'd like to find an artist who could paint it sometime. Anyway, I picture a quiet lake, and in the lake there's a boat that's tied to the dock. That's all you see at first. But then, when you move back from the picture, you see that the dock isn't attached to shore. It's floating out there in the middle of the lake along with the boat. That's our society. We've tied our lives to the dock, but the dock isn't tied to anything."

I blinked.

Whoa.

He handed me my books. "Enjoy."

∼

When I was growing up, my parents took me to church faithfully week after week every Sunday from the time I learned how to breathe. For this I am both deeply indebted and deeply scarred. A kid can only take hearing about Jonah and the whale so many times before he starts wishing the whale would just digest the guy and get it over with.

We attended a denomination where the pastors and denominational leaders were very concerned about getting their doctrine right. Over the years this denomination had split off from quite a number of other church bodies whenever those groups did things that they considered too liberal or too doctrinally impure. I was taught that for another person to be "in fellowship" with me, we needed to be in complete agreement about all matters of faith, which basically meant that she had to belong to our denomination too. If she didn't, we weren't supposed to worship with each other, share the Lord's Supper, or even say meal prayers together. And I couldn't be all too sure about seeing her in heaven one day either.

At the time, the way the pastors explained their theological distinctives to me, the issues seemed terribly important. But now, looking back, it all seems petty and nitpicky and tragic. After all, Jesus didn't come as a theological policeman wielding a carefully worded doctrinal statement;

he came as a lover to woo his bride. And throughout his career he spent a lot more time emphasizing sound living than sound teaching. But I only discovered this stuff recently. I didn't know that as a kid.

So as I fumbled my way through childhood to my teen years, God seemed distant and cold and unapproachable and very, very stern—like an angry intergalactic librarian ready to shush you for making too much noise or kick you out if you got a little too rowdy.

Then, as a college senior, I met Jesus at a small charismatic church that worshiped on the campus of Southern Illinois University. I discovered Jesus didn't have his arms folded across his chest like I'd thought but was holding them wide open instead. That year I walked into his embrace and buried my face against his shoulder and found that the cloth of his robe is softer than anything else on the planet.

After I graduated from college, I went to work for the denomination of my childhood as the program director at one of their summer camps. As part of my job, I had to take several courses on Christian doctrine from one of the denomination's approved colleges so that I could become certified to serve in ministry. I had no idea my newfound faith would clash so much with my childhood theology.

My coursework involved reading doctrinal essays written long ago by people with indecipherable German names and then filling in blanks on my worksheets with the proper words. It was like elementary school busywork all over again, only this time on religious steroids. My professor wanted to make sure we knew all the "right" answers, which meant that he didn't provide any time for discussion, exploration, mystery, doubt, questioning, or curiosity. His was a fill-in-the-blanks theology. I have my suspicions that answers-based teaching is the safest kind for a teacher. And the most suffocating kind for a learner.

During that time I heard that at our denomination's college where men trained to become pastors, the administration didn't let the students meet together for small group Bible study. I wrote to the president of the college and asked him why that was. He wrote back that they wanted to avoid "the dangers of small group Bible study." In reply, I pointed out that in the book of Acts, believers met for small group Bible study and that not studying the Bible was more dangerous than studying it, regardless of the size of the group.

He chose not to be my pen pal anymore after that.

Eventually, as you've probably guessed, my journey of faith led me away from that church body and toward a new chapter of my life. That, of course, brought a whole new set of difficulties—holding onto my faith (or perhaps discovering it) apart from religion.

Since I'd spent so many years studying biblical facts without consciously making any effort to follow Jesus, my view of Christianity had become completely distorted. It was like staring at God through the wrong end of a telescope. Rather than being about the glorious news of new life and a personal invitation into the story of God, my religion had become a matter of knowing the right answers to multiple choice questions.

I felt like my teachers had skewered the truth on a stick and fed it to me one carefully seasoned slice at a time. And it never did taste right, because it wasn't right. You might be able to serve up facts that way, but you can't do it with the truth. Facts will always leave you empty; truth will leave you full. Most people begin to choke on facts after a while, but truth is as fresh as the handshake from a friend. I know that now, because I've finally met Truth for myself.

what a desperate time it was
in the days of the dragon's curse
when the king's refrain was as still as stone,
    and all knew that soon, of course,
the land would ring with the wizard's rhyme
and the venom of his verse.

what a terrible one he was
when i first met the son of the king.
with fire in his eyes and a bladed heart
    and an ancient flute to bring
the tune of time to the throats of those
who had never learned to sing.

what a furious warring raged
when the prince went to battle the foe.
with velvet strength and a dagger of love
    and his crimson blood to flow,
the day he died the moon stood still
and the shadows gnawed my soul.

what a terrifying sight to see
a prince once dead, now strong.
with glistening tears and outstretched wings
    and a furious, glorious song.
a new day dawned and the wizard fell
and the dragon's curse was gone.

We all tie the boats of our lives to something. Sometimes it's culture, sometimes feelings, sometimes our own "personal values system." But too often we find the very dock we've relied on is floating aimlessly with us away from shore. Pascal put it this way: "We must have a fixed point in order to judge. The harbour decides for those who are in a ship; but where shall we find a harbour in morality?"[1] Or as C. S. Lewis wrote, "Where ancient man felt himself guided through an immense cathedral, modern man feels adrift on a shoreless sea."[2]

Truth is a slippery thing to talk about in our postmodern world. I know that. Life seems awfully shoreless most of the time. And now, as I look back at my childhood, I can understand that my pastors were trying to help me tie my boat to the truth—and that's a good thing. But they'd forgotten something essential about Christianity: we are made for more than the shore. We are also meant to cross the sea of mystery and explore the far side of the world.

In my heart of hearts I'm a storyteller, so only when I began to see the richness and wonder of the Jesus story did my imagination finally catch up with my intellect. Only then was true faith born.

Jesus is truth and more than truth.

He is mystery and more than mystery.

He is the shore I can count on. And he is the sail filled with an eager and restless wind.

He is both.

Here's what I've learned: finding the right dock is not about discovering the right answer but about encountering the right person. When I began to look closely at the words of Jesus for myself, I realized that truth isn't an idea, or a concept, or a philosophical construct at all. Truth isn't a dogma to be believed but a person to be known. Truth is love dressed in skin. Jesus is the Truth; the Truth is Jesus.

"I am the way, the truth, and the life," he told his disciples (John 14:6). So truth has a human heart and speaks with a human tongue. Jesus doesn't just know the truth; he himself *is* the living, breathing, freeing truth. And knowing the truth, knowing Jesus, sets us free (see John 8:31–32). He is at the same time the truth that's taught and the Truth who is known—truth to be submitted to and, ultimately, truth to be reckoned with.

When I first discovered this concept, I thought of printing up a bunch of T-shirts that said "Truth has a belly button" on the front and "John 14:6" on the back. I thought maybe they'd be great discussion starters. "Truth has a belly button?" people would ask. "What's that supposed to mean?" And I could tell them the story about the day Truth was born and laid in a manger.

But I'm kind of shy in small groups and not very good at talking to strangers, so I never did get them printed. If you like the idea, be my guest. You don't even have to give me credit for the idea. Sell them on eBay. Make some money. Start a revolution.

∾

This whole notion that truth is a person is very refreshing to me, and a little bit freeing, and somewhat disturbing. It rocks my world but also stirs something deep within me, a hungry part of my soul that was starving for a long time. Knowing the right facts isn't how you get to know the truth; knowing Jesus is.

This is also why so many theological experts have such vacant souls—because knowledge alone doesn't free us. It traps us between jagged facts, while simple faith in Jesus is the pathway to the real. And that's why Paul could write, "Your real life is hidden with Christ in God" (Colossians 3:3). Jesus is my new life, my real life, and my truest identity comes through knowing him. The deepest realities of life can only be found in the hands of the tale-spinning rabbi.

In the end, the question at the heart of Christianity is not "Who do I want to be?" but "Whose do I want to become—my own or his?"

the carpenter picks up the saw
and walks toward me again.
i shudder and gasp, "why?
why is he torturing me like this?"
but then, after the blade
has done its work, i realize that
in the hands of a master carpenter,
no piece of wood is safe
　　from becoming a masterpiece.

Now, I know that all this talk about truth can make some people uneasy. After all, truth can seem very theoretical and philosophical and not all that relevant or relational. But the freeing aspect of Jesus's teachings is this: truth cannot be known simply with your head; it must be known with your life. We can only discover the authentically true life by following a first-century carpenter.

It seems to me that in our culture today, some people (usually those of us over thirty-five) are comfortable talking about truth. "Jesus is the answer," we sing around the campfire, "for the world today! Above him there's no other. Jesus is the way!" To us, Jesus is an answer.

But the younger generation (let's say, seventeen to thirty-four) isn't looking for answers. They're not even sure answers exist. All they want is someone to walk with them through this tangled journey of tears and pain and laughter we call life. They're suspicious of those who make truth claims. It seems arrogant or imperialistic to claim to know the truth in our pluralistic society. Instead of certainty, most of my friends this age are hungry for relational integrity, transcendence, community, wonder, mystery, story. This view of life is what people often refer to as postmodernism.

The astounding thing about Jesus is that he's able to give both groups what they're hungry for, while at the same time challenging each of us to explore the facets of truth and mystery that make us uneasy. The Carpenter of Hearts provides both ultimate truth and supreme mystery without diluting either. We can both rest in the cove of his love and sail farther than we'd ever hoped to go.

∾

When we get caught up debating our philosophical differences—*Do moral absolutes exist, or is morality a series of shades of gray? Is truth personal or universal? In a universe where even time is relative, how can you be certain about anything?*—Jesus stands on the sidelines and shouts, "You're both barking up the wrong tree, amigos! Truth isn't a philosophical idea or concept. Stop trying to define it and start letting it (me!) define you."

> borrowed sunglasses
> help me to see
> the world through
> another's eyes.
> yet, when i slip yours on,
> the day seems brighter,
> not darker
> than before.

Paul calls Jesus "the mystery of God" (Colossians 2:2 NIV). Most of the time I tend to picture truth and mystery as lying on different ends of a continuum, but Jesus reveals that they're simply opposite facets of the same thing—God's love made real in the world. Mystery and truth lie in the same direction and the same place—within the heart of a man born in a stable.

He is truth wrapped in mystery, wonder wrapped in love.

For a long time my life was adrift, but when I discovered where to lash my boat, I finally found a dock that would not float away, as well as a sail that would take me into the deepest waters of life.

good things running wild

In college I studied recreation (I know that sounds like an oxymoron) and spent my summers working at YMCA camps in Minnesota and Wisconsin. During the last week of the summer before my junior year, I was volunteering as an activity leader at a family camp in northern Minnesota.

After a long day of leading games and skits, I curled up with a book in my cabin. Outside, the night was cool and a bit breezy. I could hear the loons calling across the interconnected network of lakes that separate Minnesota from Canada. The haunting cry of a loon somehow sounds lonely and at home, wild and familiar, all at the same time. It can be chilling.

I was sitting on the edge of a couch near the open window, reading a collection of short stories penned by fiction-writing vegetarian activists. I'd just finished a story about a cow who escaped the slaughterhouse and eventually made her way back to the farm to warn the others of the bloody terrors in store for them, but of course they didn't believe her tales of torturous death, and then, with a taut dramatic plunge, the story ended when the nice-looking, calm-talking men showed up at the barn with their cattle truck. It seems a little lame now that I write about it, but at the time it was pretty much freaking me out. Especially with the loons calling outside my window.

As I finished up the chapter about the enlightened cow, I heard a voice whisper my name from just outside the cabin window. Startled, I almost dropped the book. All I could think of was those nice-looking, calm-talking men with their cattle truck. I leaned toward the window, hesitantly, until I saw who was standing there. "Hollywood?" I said. "What are you doing?"

I have no idea what his real name was. The girls working at the camp had nicknamed him Hollywood because he had the winning smile, strong chin, and chiseled chest of a big screen leading man. Hollywood was my age, tanned and toned (of course), in charge of the sailing program (of course), and wore sunglasses all day (of course). He defined cool at that camp.

He was smiling. "Wanna go sailing?"

"What are you talking about?" I set down the book and glanced at my watch. It was almost midnight.

"Sailing, you know. It's awesome at night."

"Isn't it against the rules?"

Hollywood shrugged. "It'll be okay. Besides, I'm in charge of the sail-boats, remember? Come on." Then he took a step backward, showing me both that he expected me to come and that he wouldn't wait forever.

Part of me was certain there must be some kind of rule against sailing at night, that I'd be caught by the camp director and get into Big Trouble. But then again, what would he do, fire me? I was only a volunteer, and I'd be leaving in three days anyway. And besides, Hollywood *was* the guy in charge of the sailboats . . .

"Okay," I said at last. "Sounds cool."

"Right on."

I turned off the lights and slipped outside. The smell of ancient firs and smoldering campfires greeted me. The sky was alive with stars.

Hollywood led me along the trail to the dock. I was still a little nervous about the idea, but as we neared the water, the thrill of adventure began to drown out the fear of getting caught. I was actually going sailing at midnight with the cool guy.

Hollywood stepped lithely onto one of the sailboats and motioned for me to join him. Then he asked if I knew how to sail.

I shook my head.

"It's easy." Then Hollywood explained how to position the sails to take advantage of the wind, and how to angle the boat into the waves to increase your speed, and where to sit to best distribute your weight when you're turning. He made the complex physics of it sound amazingly simple and natural, just like all great teachers intuitively know how to do. Then he untied the boat, and my fears resurfaced. "Um, what if we hit an island or something?"

"I know where the islands are."

"What if we hit a sandbar?"

"We'll stay in the deep water." And then the boat was free of the dock. "Trust me."

Stars gleamed high above us while their reflections rippled in the water below. As we eased forward into the night, it was almost like we were sailing between the stars.

Once we were out of the secluded cove, the wind kicked up and Hollywood guided us past the islands and through the Milky Way. Sometimes he would lean way out over the lake and laugh as the water sprayed into his face. I held on tightly at first, still thinking we were going to capsize, but when I realized I wasn't going to drown in the middle of the Minnesotan night, I loosened my grip and began to enjoy my ride through the galaxy.

And sometimes, on the lee side of an island when the wind was still and the water was calm, we would rock silently between the stars and talk about girls and college and dreams of the future. And everything seemed right in the world.

~

A number of years after that midnight sail, I went on a thirteen-day solo hike through the Wind River Range, an isolated wilderness in Wyoming. On day seven I rested by a glacial lake 10,421 feet above sea level because my toes were badly bruised from wearing boots that were too small. I spent my day of rest soaking my feet and reading poetry and then, at twilight, watching fish jump out of the clear water and rise, if only for a moment, 10,422 feet above the level of the sea.

I started wondering what it would be like to be one of those fish, swimming through this mountain lake minding my own business and then one day rising to the ceiling of all that there is and finding that I could poke my nose through the surface of the sky. And not only my nose but to learn, in a moment of glorious discovery, that with the right flip of my tail I could break through the rippling curtain of my world and take flight, experiencing the strange and wonderful and dangerous freedom of the air.

I imagined I might swim back to the others and tell them about the new world I'd discovered—a place too magnificent for the language of fish to describe. I wondered if they would believe me. After all, sometimes news is too terrible to believe—that's why the cows laughed at their friend. But sometimes we don't believe because the news is just too incredible.

At first I thought it was somehow unnatural for fish to jump like that: *They're fish, right? They're just supposed to swim in the water. After all, that's what they're made for.* But as night fell and the stars began to bespeckle the sky, I realized that for a fish to leave the water isn't breaking the rules at all—it's just exploring the true extent of what it really means to be a fish.

Of course fish are made for the water. Of course they're made to swim.

But they're also made to jump.

In the days of Jesus, the religious leaders thought that living a godly life meant following a set of carefully constructed rules. They had camp rulebook theology: if you follow the guidelines closely enough, you'll be okay, but if you break too many of them, you'll be in Big Trouble. Forever. And no one gets to go sailing at midnight. Period.

So then here comes Jesus, showing great respect for God, calling people to a purity that went way beyond the constraints of the religious laws, yet at the same time teaching about a way of life that culminated in unbridled compassion and freedom. As he said himself, "If the Son sets you free, you will be free indeed" (John 8:36 NIV).

The enigma of his theology bothered the religious purists—on the one hand, he certainly spoke and acted and taught like someone straight from God's head office, but on the other hand, he didn't seem all that concerned about keeping their nitpicky rules. And that bothered them to no end.

Then one day they had their chance to nail him. Jesus was walking through a grain field with his disciples on the designated day of rest (the Sabbath day). On the way, his disciples began to break off some of the wheat and munch on it as they hiked. So the Pharisees confronted Jesus, claiming that his friends were harvesting on the Sabbath day—a great big no-no for the Jews. I can just hear them: "No picking of trail snacks on Saturday! It clearly says so right here on page 1172 of the rulebook, right next to the regulations about how to wash your stew pots!"

Jesus just shook his head. "The Sabbath was made for man," he told them, "and not man for the Sabbath. And I, the Son of Man, am Lord even of the Sabbath!" (see Mark 2:27–28).

His buddies were hungry. Sure, picking the grain might have been against a fundamentalist interpretation of the Jewish law, but having a bite to eat certainly wasn't against God's bylaws. And to prove his point, Jesus chose one of the Pharisees' favorite heroes, King David, and explained how he and his soldiers had broken the rules too by eating special bread reserved for the priests. Jesus didn't excuse either David's behavior or his own disciples' but rather used this opportunity to explain that there's actually something more important than keeping the rules—regulations are superseded by the priority of being fully human.

∾

After becoming a believer, I spent years as a camp rulebook Christian. Then one day when I read Jesus's words about the Sabbath, it struck me that I wasn't made to follow the rules, I was made to follow Jesus. And that realization led me to this one—it almost sounds sacrilegious to say it, but here it is: God is more concerned with us doing what is good than with us doing what is right.

Once when Jesus healed a crippled woman on a Sabbath day, the synagogue leader was indignant. "Come during the week to get healed," he told the people, "not on the Sabbath!" But then Jesus explained that doing good, showing compassion, and saving a life are never against the rules:

> The Lord replied, "You hypocrite! You work on the Sabbath day! Don't you untie your ox or your donkey from their stalls on the Sabbath and lead them out for water? Wasn't it necessary for me, even on the Sabbath day, to free this dear woman from the bondage in which Satan has held her for eighteen years?"
>
> This shamed his enemies. And all the people rejoiced at the wonderful things he did.
>
> Luke 13:15–17

Jesus told them it was *necessary* for him to free the woman; the day of the week had no authority over his compassion. Often the right question is not "What does the law require?" but "What does love require?" The law might require rest, but love requires compassion. And when love is properly lived out, it fulfills all that the law could ever ask.

How can you fault someone for rescuing, healing, freeing, forgiving, making restitution—on any day of the week? On any day of your life? The people rejoiced at Jesus's words because he brought freedom to this woman and showed the duplicity of the fundamentalists. I like how Paul puts it: "The fruit of the Spirit is love, joy, peace, patience, kindness, goodness, faithfulness, gentleness and self-control. *Against such things there is no law*" (Galatians 5:22–23 NIV, emphasis added). The minute you try to reign them in, you've steered away from the ways of God.

People weren't created for the benefit of the rules; instead, rules were created to benefit us as we aim our lives toward God. That day at the wheat fields, the religious fundamentalists were using the Sabbath rest to intimidate, control, and frighten the people. At other times they used their many other religious rules to do the same. Then here comes Jesus, explaining that when rules get in the way of the life of love, freedom, compassion, and justice, those rules are no longer enforceable on a divine scale.

I'd read this wheat-picking story lots of times, even heard sermons on it, but only recently did I begin to understand how radical this teaching is. The day of rest was made for us, not the other way around. When God rested on the seventh day of creation, he didn't do it for himself but for us. He wasn't resting because he was tired; he was still creating. Only this time he was doing it by example, modeling a day of rest for his children. He rested because we need it, not because he does.

The point of establishing a day of rest was to help us renew our day-to-day relational encounter with the holy. Because without that time of rest and reflection, we become addicted to work and distracted by our urgent, busy, nitpicky lives. When that happens, we slowly wear our souls away to raw little nubs as we become less and less human. That's what was happening to the Pharisees. That's what happens to us today.

But Jesus twisted his tail and rose, glistening in the sun, as the other fish tried to explain the rules of the water to him. "Don't you see," he tells them, "you weren't just made for the water; you were made to explore the sky!"

Life in the kingdom of God means sometimes rising out of the water into a whole different way of living. A life where mystery and truth kiss in the twilight.

Somewhere along the line, the notions of Christianity, the church, and "being a believer" have become a set of rules both spoken and unspoken about how a good Christian should act, dress, worship, serve, give, study, pray, and talk. Praise God. Amen. Hallelujah, brother! But Jesus is here to show us how to sail beyond both literalism and liberalism to a life that's more true and freeing than either.

I don't think God is too concerned with whether or not I change the oil or go to my daughter's soccer game or check out a movie on my day of rest. I think part of the freedom of new life is finding creative ways to celebrate his love and his gifts on every day of the week.

> no, i do not think that God is in the
> business of collapsing our dreams.
> rather he unfolds them, smoothing
> out the wrinkles with his steady,
> weathered hands. he doesn't confine
> us in rigid rituals and demands
> but opens the soul gate grandly,
> and frees us like
> calves
> at dawn,
> to leap across the open-gated
> oneness of his meadow.

The unprecedented thing about Jesus was that he never undermined the laws. In fact, he even used the whetstone of the Sermon on the Mount to sharpen them enough to prick anyone's conscience. Instead of diminishing the importance of God's laws, Jesus came to fulfill them and put them into perspective. He didn't come with an eraser to obliterate the old laws but with the fresh ink of God's love to complete them.

When it came to matters of the heart, to matters of purity and devotion, Jesus called people to a deeper holiness than ever before: "The law might say not to murder," he told them, "but I say not to hate. Sure, the law says 'an eye for an eye,' but I say don't resist an evil person at all." Then he pinpointed pure motives as the key ingredients in prayer and giving and redefined adultery to include not just physical intimacy but also emotional and imaginational seductions as well (see Matthew 5–6).

How do we make sense of this man who teaches and lives complete freedom *as well as* total integrity?

In his book *Orthodoxy*, G. K. Chesterton explored his own journey toward faith (yes, the Hawaiian bookseller was right, it is a good book). One of the paradoxes Chesterton noticed was that Christianity did not allow a person to be partly angry and partly kind to criminals. Instead, it taught that we must treat the crime with severity (justice) and the criminal with forgiveness (love). He wrote, "We must be much more angry with theft than before, and yet much kinder to thieves than before. There was room for wrath and love to run wild. And the more I considered Christianity, the more I found that while it had established a rule and order, the chief aim of that order was to give room for good things to run wild."[1] This is the doctrine of the wind tugging at your hair and the untamed cry of a loon echoing through the night.

This idea that Christianity is about good things running wild is central to the teachings of Jesus and is splashed all throughout the New Testament, yet somehow it never seems to find its way into modern sermons anymore. We seem to be in support of the "good" part, but the "wild" part makes most pastors a little uneasy. Yet Jesus is here to set us free and show us the heart of God—and God's heart is not riddled with rules; it's saturated with love.

And so the Lord of Sailing knocks at our window and says, "C'mon! Sail with me through the night. It'll be awesome! Trust me on this. The wind is kicking up and the stars are all out and I know where the deep water flows. What do you say?"

And he steps onto the boat and extends his hand to help us climb aboard.

∽

It seems most Christians (including me) are quick to explain away Jesus's calls to true discipleship but slow to give up our religious and denominational baggage. That's where my struggle is these days.

Following Jesus isn't just a matter of choosing right from wrong. Living according to rules is easy compared to living according to love. And sometimes love must break the rules because it answers to a higher authority. "Now the Lord is the Spirit, and where the Spirit of the Lord is, there is freedom" (2 Corinthians 3:17 NIV). This isn't easy for me to wrap my mind around because I prefer straight lines and easy solutions and stock answers and easy-to-understand theology. I prefer rules to freedom.

At least I used to. But lately I've been letting his truth run wild in my heart. He navigates through the night, laughing as the water sprays into his face. And slowly, finally, I'm beginning to nose out of the water and twist my tail. Ready, at last, to jump.

joy on the front of my pants

A few years ago my pastor asked me to speak for the Sunday morning service at our church. I titled my message "Getting ReJOYvenated." I'll admit I was feeling a little smug about my clever little title, right up to my drive to church when I realized my talk wasn't nearly as engaging as the title was. I had prepared a lecture on joy that wouldn't even keep me awake.

So I started frantically trying to think of some way to make the message more memorable. Then I drove past a grocery store and had a brainstorm, or at least a brain-sprinkle. I jogged inside and bought four bottles of Joy concentrated dishwashing liquid—three little bottles and one mongo-sized one.

When I arrived at church, I went into the church kitchen and grabbed a large bowl and the biggest knife they had. When I stood up to speak, I set the bowl on a stool in the middle of the stage, and after introducing the theme of my message, I pulled out one of the small bottles of Joy and the carving knife. "Now, if I do this," I told the people, "I don't want anyone to accuse me of being a killjoy." A few people actually laughed. Some of the three-piece-suit-wearing church members grabbed the comment cards and started furiously scribbling.

Then, as I talked about all the things that drain joy from our lives—anger, resentment, worry, guilt, shame, regrets, and so on—I stabbed the bottle of Joy in my best imitation of Norman Bates in the shower scene from *Psycho*. I was rather enthusiastic in my impersonation. It was great, although I think I scared some of the people in the front row.

Then I held up the punctured bottle of Joy and squeezed it. Joy came oozing—or in some cases squirting—out of the stab wounds. Some of it landed in the bowl on the stool, but more than I anticipated went spurting across the stage. A couple of women grabbed their purses and held them up like shields. About then I was feeling much less anxious than I'd been on the way to church. The stabbing and squeezing and oozing was very therapeutic, actually. And a lot less costly than counseling.

At last I talked about how God's joy is available to each one of us, and I pulled out the great big bottle of Joy and poured it into the small, mortally wounded bottle while I quoted Bible verses that showed God's desire to share his joy with us. "Listen," I said, "our God is a God of joy, and he wants to pour that joy into your life. Psalm 30:11 says God clothes us with joy. Psalm 45:7 says he anoints our heads with the oil of joy—he clothes us with joy, he drenches us with joy!" The women in the front row nodded in agreement. "Psalm 126:3 says he fills us with joy. Isaiah 35:10 says he overwhelms us with joy and crowns our heads with it. How would you like to be clothed, drenched, filled, overwhelmed, and crowned with joy?"

By then the punctured bottle was overflowing with fresh Joy, and I'd made my point. I finished by talking about the different ways God infuses joy back into our lives through his promises, his story, his Spirit, his love, stuff like that.

The first service ended, and I was feeling pretty good about how well everything had gone. I headed into the church kitchen to clean up the knife and the bowl and to get ready for the next service, and as I was pouring water into the bowl to rinse out the Joy, some of the Joy splashed onto the front of my pants.

I was wearing light brown khakis that day. Needless to say, it didn't look like Joy on the front of my pants. It looked an awful lot like something else.

So I did what seemed sensible at the time. I tried to wash off the Joy.

Now, to someone who doesn't normally do the dishes, the word *concentrate* means "to focus your attention." It does not mean "to foam up your pants." So the more I scrubbed the front of my pants, the less it looked like Joy down there. I'd been drenched with Joy all right, but I wasn't so sure it was from the Lord.

After a few minutes I realized that washing my pants wasn't working too well at all, so I tried to use some paper towels to dry them off. But the paper towels didn't soak up the Joy like I'd hoped. Instead, they just pretty much spread it out more evenly across the zipper area of my trousers.

I looked at my watch. Twenty minutes remained before the next service began, and I knew I couldn't stand up in front of the congregation like that. I was getting desperate. I even tried the hand dryer in the bathroom, but the heat was, well, a bit unsettling on that area of my anatomy.

Finally I untucked my shirt to cover the Joy, slouched over so no one would notice my little accident, and started walking around the lobby of our church, going up to guys who looked about my size saying, "Excuse me, I'm preaching today. Could I borrow your pants?"

I'm six-foot-three, so it was tough to find people who were tall enough to help. It was even tougher to find a guy who wanted to swap outfits with me.

By then the start of the next service was only ten minutes away, and I realized I wasn't going to find anyone my size who would be willing to wear my wet pair of pants while I stood up in front of the church and preached to him wearing his dry pair.

The only option left was to drive home, change clothes, and try to make it back by the time my talk was supposed to start. The congregation would be singing three songs to begin the service, so if I hurried I just might make it.

My house is about twelve minutes from the church—that is, if you drive like a Christian and there are no traffic jams or retired couples heading to Florida in their new Winnebago in front of you. As I hopped into the car I figured I had maybe eighteen minutes total to get home, change, and get back to the service before I had to step up front to speak about joy. All that said, I admit that I drove through our town at a rate of speed that was, well, biblically incorrect.

The whole way I pictured getting pulled over by a police officer. "Excuse me, sir. Yes, um—what's this stain on my pants? Well, you see, I had a little accident back at church. Yes, I spilled some of my joy. Wanna come hear me preach?"

Thankfully, I made it home without a speeding ticket. I raced inside, grabbed a pair of pants, pulled them on, and jumped back into the car. As I zipped up these pants, I realized they were too small around the waist. But by then I had no choice. I had to wear them.

As I was driving back to church, I glanced at the gas gauge in the car.

Now, I know that by now you're probably thinking that I have to be making this stuff up. I know I'd be thinking that if I were you. But sometimes real life is so odd that it wouldn't make a good novel. In fiction, things have to at least be believable. But real life isn't governed by the same set of rules. So, yes, the gas gauge was hovering a few degrees below zero. Celsius. At that point I remembered one of the Bible verses I'd uncovered while researching joy: "Consider it pure joy, my brothers, whenever you face trials of many kinds" (James 1:2 NIV). I just sat there staring at the gas gauge, trying not to suffocate in the pants that were too tight for me, while speeding crazily through town thinking, *I am so !@#$% joyful right now!*

I made it to the church, pulled into the parking lot, and ran inside. The congregation was singing the last verse of the joyful song that preceded my joyful message. I took a deep breath, straightened out my shirt, sucked in my gut so I could actually keep my pants buttoned, cleared my throat, and walked onto the platform to stab a bottle of dishwashing liquid in front of seven hundred people who just wanted to reconnect with the joy of God again.

Most of the time, joy—true joy, genuine joy—seems just out of reach to me. It seems like something that lands on my shoulder for a moment, like a curious butterfly, but then flaps away as soon as I try to close my fingers around it so I can take it home and put it in a jar and set it on my desk forever. It comes in unlikely moments and in untidy ways. I leap toward it, finger it, but can't quite hold on.

In those rare instances when I actually do find joy, I always hope it's just the beginning of something more, of a new way of life. But then, when I've barely sunk my teeth into it, it's gone all over again, fleeting in the night.

> grain by grain the sand passes
> through my moments, piling onto
> the fragile slopes of my days.
>   who will tip the hourglass over
> and give my life another shot
> at glory?

I know there are lots of theological reasons for all this: that we're fallen creatures with tarnished souls; that in the original plan we were meant to experience joy completely, but our first parents fumbled the ball in the Garden of Eden and we haven't recovered much yardage in all the years since.

I know all these things in my head, but frankly, it doesn't help me much when the kids are whining or I sprain my ankle or my friend tells me what she really thinks of my latest book. Because I really do want more joy in my life. I really do want more fullness and peace, but my circumstances always seem to keep getting in the way.

There's a story in the Old Testament about a guy named Nehemiah who travels to Jerusalem to oversee the rebuilding of the walls surrounding the city, which have been demolished for years. After a series of misadventures and setbacks, sabotage attempts and death threats, the walls are finally completed. (It's a great story, actually. Worth checking out if you've never read it. It's found in Nehemiah 2–6.)

Then the people of the city gather together to hear Ezra the priest read from the Book of the Law. As they listen to him explain the commands and promises of God, the Israelites begin to weep. At that point, Nehemiah stands up and says, "Don't weep on such a day as this! For today is a sacred day before the LORD your God. . . . Go and celebrate with a feast of choice foods and sweet drinks, and share gifts of food with people who have nothing prepared. This is a sacred day before our Lord. Don't be dejected and sad, for the joy of the LORD is your strength!" (Nehemiah 8:9–10).

I like how, in Nehemiah's eyes, a sacred day meant one of selfless celebration, with "choice food and sweet drinks." To Nehemiah, sad, heavy hearts clashed with sacredness. According to him, it's sacred to party. That's such a healthy, refreshing view of holiness. And then he closes by telling the people that the joy of the Lord is their strength.

I used to read that and wonder why it didn't say, "The strength of the Lord is your joy." I thought that would have made more sense. I mean, the people were weeping and needed to find joy again in their relationship with God. I would've thought Nehemiah would emphasize how powerful God is and that his power can give them joy once again. That would seem sensible.

But nope. Instead Nehemiah said, "The joy of the Lord is your strength."

I asked a pastor about this verse one time, and he looked it up in the Hebrew. "The word that's translated 'strength' here is the same word that's translated throughout the rest of the book as 'wall,'" he told me. "It literally means 'the joy of the Lord is your *wall*.'"

"So it's a play on words?" I said.

"Sort of. The point is, it's a wall."

"It's a pun!" I said. As a writer I'm way too easily impressed by literary devices.

"No, it's a wall."

"Right, and a pun!"

He sighed and walked away. I tend to have that effect on people. I did thank him, however, even though I wasn't exactly sure I understood the subtle significance of his translation. I had to think about it for a while.

Don't be dejected and sad, for the joy of the Lord is your wall.

The people were celebrating the completion of their city walls, walls built to hold out their enemies and provide them with protection and security. So all around them stood these walls they could see, that they'd helped to build. And here comes Nehemiah pointing out a different wall, one they couldn't see, especially through their tears. This was a wall built out of sacred joy rather than sweat and rocks and mortar and time.

I think I finally get it: a wall built out of God's joy can hold back the greatest enemies of all.

I have a theory that there are two types of people. One group is the Morning People. We all know who they are. They're easy to identify, with their big shiny teeth and enthusiastic handshakes and peppy Time To Go Do Yoga And Greet The Day! speeches.

Most of us are the other group. No, we're not Evening People or even Afternoon People. We're Anti-Morning People. You probably know right off the bat which group you belong to.

One summer I was in Atlanta, riding an elevator down to the hotel lobby at 7:30 a.m., when a smartly dressed African-American woman stepped aboard.

"And how are you doing today?" she asked me brightly.

"Good," I mumbled. For me, at that time of day even speaking was a notable accomplishment. "How are you?"

She beamed. "MIRACULOUSLY FABULOUS, BLESSED, AND HIGHLY FAVORED!"

I had to put my hand against the side of the elevator to steady myself. I think my heart might actually have stopped. You can't talk that way to an Anti-Morning Person at 7:30 a.m. You have to be gentle with us until about midafternoon or so. She looked at me with a sly grin. "Woke you up, didn't I?"

I felt my pulse to make sure I was still alive. "Um, yeah."

Then the elevator doors slid open and she stepped out to meet her friends, who were waiting at the other end of the lobby. "AND HOW ARE YOU SAINTS DOIN' THIS MORNING?" she shouted.

I had actually met the Queen Mother of all Morning Persons and survived.

After I speak at conferences, people sometimes ask me how it went. "Um, okay," I usually say. I'm not sure how to respond. I wonder what it would have been like if the disciples had asked Jesus that question after he was done preaching. "So, Jesus, how did it go?"

"Well," he says, "some people argued with me and then tried to arrest me. A big chunk of the audience walked out in the middle of my sermon, and the rest of the people picked up stones to kill me. But other than that, I'd say it went pretty well."

Honestly, I don't really like it when people ask me how things are going. I wish we had a better greeting in America than "Hey! How ya doin'?" All too often I have big areas of life scratching at the back of my brain that I wish I could mention—some good, some bad—but of course I don't say anything about them. I just say, "I'm good. How are you?"

∽

Time for a little self-revelation.

Like a number of people I know, I've struggled at certain times of my life with depression. I wish I could actually explain how rough it can be, but it's tough to put into words. Stuff you used to love doing becomes merely endurable. Just carrying on everyday conversations with people can wear you out. Food doesn't taste good. Even the things you really enjoy—chicken cordon bleu and Kit Kat bars and big, juicy, char-grilled, medium-rare cheeseburgers—taste like paste.

Work becomes a looming, frightening thing set before you each day, tedious and tiring. But as tired as you get during the day, you can't seem to sleep at night. And the lack of sleep only makes things worse. You feel guilty and shameful and desperate and isolated and very much alone. Prayer doesn't always help. And most of the time, God's love seems just out of reach.

One day when I was depressed I went on a walk and realized I couldn't think of anything in the future I was looking forward to. No movies I wanted to see, no books I wanted to read (or write), no speaking engagements I was excited about, no family vacations on the horizon that I thought I'd enjoy. My entire future seemed infinitely bleak and meaningless. I can tell you, feeling like there's nothing in life to look forward to is one of the scariest feelings in the world.

When you're depressed, it's harder and harder to care about the things that used to matter. And sometimes you just break into tears and can't stop crying. Of course, you do your best to hide it, to wait until you're alone before you lose it. But people can see you're on the verge of tears, so they ask you how you're doing and you get tired of acting happy and saying, "I'm good. How are you?" because you realize after a few times of telling them how you're really doing that they don't exactly want to hear all that because it makes them feel awkward. So you retreat into yourself and your desperate, lonely world, and that only makes things worse.

And sometimes you get to a point where you don't even want to be alive anymore. You just want to give up and get it over with. Once when I was feeling like that, I wrote this:

> i keep pouring more ingredients into my life
> pulling from the lives of others
> and the dreams i used to have
> to find the right emotions to mix into my stew.
>   "wait till you taste how i turn out!" i say
>   "just you wait and see!"
> but hope keeps drifting further
> into the mist and i just can't
> seem to get the flavor right and
> no matter how many more spices
> i add, every spoonful of my life
> still tastes like yesterday's tears.

I remember driving toward the park one day when I was feeling really low. Up ahead I saw a bridge abutment for the overpass. I remember thinking, *I can't think of any good reason not to drive this car off the road and slam it into that cement piling thing.*

The closer I came to the overpass, the stronger the urge became, until I began to edge the wheels off the highway and they spit up stones that clattered against the underside of the car. For some reason that sound jolted me back to my senses, and I eased back into my lane on the highway. No one ever knew.

I've seen other people swerve out of their lanes at odd times. Most of the time it's probably because they spilled some coffee, or they're yelling at the kids in the backseat, or maybe they're just busy talking on the cell phone. But I wonder if sometimes the swerving means something else.

∾

There aren't any easy answers to the big questions that haunt us and hunt us down. Friends commit suicide. Grandparents die awkwardly and alone in nursing homes. We get fired. We have affairs. Our kids get hooked on drugs. Time and gravity wear us down as we travel across this vale of tears.

Yet when we have hope, we have a refuge. I like how Paul put it: "We do not lose heart. Though outwardly we are wasting away, yet inwardly we are being renewed day by day" (2 Corinthians 4:16 NIV). Or, as Eugene Peterson paraphrases it in *The Message*, "We're not giving up. How could we! Even though on the outside it often looks like things are falling apart on us, on the inside, where God is making new life, not a day goes by without his unfolding grace." And grace is always stronger than my circumstances.

Every day we're both wasting away and being renewed. When God's Spirit moves, joy is reborn, and our lives, once new, can continually be renewed through faith and the promises of faith.

Here's what I have to keep reminding myself: pain is real, but so is joy. Every moment, hope is available. Even now, peace can be mine. And the sparkling moments of joy that make life worth living are just as much a part of our world as the speeding tickets and funerals. When you take the time to look at both sides of the equation, you realize that life is both more depressing and more delightful than you thought.

I think it's significant that the Bible never says Jesus enjoyed suffering. Pain is no fun—at least not for healthy, emotionally stable people.

Hebrews 12:2 says we should keep our lives focused on Jesus, "who for the joy set before him endured the cross" (NIV). Jesus didn't enjoy the cross; he endured it. If you meet a Christian who acts happy all the time—that shallow, plastic kind of happiness—avoid him like the dentist after Halloween. He has one eye closed to reality.

Jesus never acted artificially happy. And despite what you may have heard from some well-meaning preacher, Jesus did not like being tortured to death. He didn't delight in it; he put up with it. To enjoy pain isn't Christianity; it's masochism. But to willingly endure suffering because you love something more than your own comfort level, well, that's getting closer to the heart of the divine.

Joy is often wedded to sorrow, peace often accentuated through pain. Christianity isn't just about putting up with hardships or dealing with problems or handling suffering. One of the paradoxes of faith is embracing those things voluntarily as a way of expressing devotion to God. Christianity is a journey that takes you everywhere you've always wanted to go but never by the route you'd expect. Or choose.

This voluntary aspect of love (and in some cases the willing acceptance of pain because of it) is one of the features of Christianity that sets it apart from other religions. Obligation and duty are not the same as love. Love offers itself. It actually volunteers for the cross.

> i want to untangle the future
> but for now i'll let
> the riddle of
> your love for me
> take me along the current
> of this moment
> as i whisper
> > my yes
> and strive to live out
> > my thanks.

In the accounts of the resurrection of Jesus, we find his friends filled with both fear and joy: "The women ran quickly from the tomb. They were very frightened but also filled with great joy, and they rushed to find the disciples to give them the angel's message" (Matthew 28:8).

I'm not sure where their fear came from. Maybe they were afraid of the Romans. Maybe they were afraid of God. I have a feeling they were afraid of the repercussions if Jesus really was alive again. After all, they hadn't believed him when he said he was going to rise again. And since his death they'd been living as if his words were lies. The enemy had slipped in past their walls and robbed them of joy. But now a greater joy—a joy from above—was unfolding before them because his words, his life, might actually be true. And it's frightening to realize Jesus might actually love you that much—that he might really be willing to endure the cross for the joy of standing by your side.

I like that there's a mixture of fear and joy in their response to the news. I get uneasy around people who pretend to be happy all the time and act as if life is one great big pep rally for Jesus. I don't think I'd survive five minutes at a convention for Morning People.

But on the other hand, I don't like it when people are gloomy and depressed all the time either. I read somewhere that St. Francis of Assisi said, "It is not fitting, when one is in God's service, to have a gloomy face or a chilling look." That's a good word from St. Francis. Of course, as far as we know, he never spilled Joy on the front of his pants.

There's a heaviness to the lightness of Christianity, a somberness to the joy, a depth to the levity, because for every Easter there is a Good Friday. We approach God with reverence and awe (see Hebrews 12:28), and we can't help but have some solemnity when standing before the judge of the universe. But at the same time, we're offered complete joy, inexpressible in its fullness and incomparable in its power. As Jesus told his followers, "As the Father has loved me, so have I loved you. Now remain in my love. . . .

I have told you this so that my joy may be in you and that your joy may be complete" (John 15:9, 11 NIV).

Christians are enmeshed in a terrible, glorious, light and airy, deep and troubling joy. Thinking about this one day led me to whisper this prayer:

> the night is as black as an eel.
> the day is as long as the night.
> my heart has been wrapped up in steel.
> i can feel the vampires bite.
>
> the tenuous leaves of the autumn!
> the trembling gates of the sky!
> my wonder is under the bottom
> of the dreams that i see floating by.
>
> o terror that trembles the treetops!
> o spinner of marvel and dread!
> let hope once again into me drop
> and awaken this soul
>   that was dead!

Jesus, the one whom Isaiah calls "a man of sorrows" (Isaiah 53:3), was also a man of complete joy. He wasn't partly sad and a little bit happy. His soul overflowed with both the pain of the world and the indescribable glory of God—at the same time. And the more we become like him, the more we will overflow with the same.

Don't ask me how all this works. I think that since Jesus was the only perfect person ever, he experienced the most extreme emotions any human has ever felt—the most extreme joy, the most intense sorrow, the greatest happiness, the deepest grief. I think if you page through the Gospels, you'll see this in his tears and anger and thanksgiving and wry jokes.

His soul is clothed in both the bloodstained fabric of the wounded warrior and the unblemished veil of a bride gleaming white in the afternoon sun. Christianity means diving into the depths of humanity, into what it really means to be fully alive, and that brings both sorrow and joy, both fear and thanksgiving.

Things are good. Things are not so good.

I'm fine. I'm not so fine.

I'm wasting away. I'm being renewed.

I'm miraculously fabulous, blessed, and highly favored. I've got Joy on the front of my pants.

I'm an agathokakological guy, thank you very much.

Christianity offers this strange mixture of sorrow and joy and hope and regret and confidence and humility—and honesty too, because when you enter the realm of grace, you enter the arena of awareness. You become acutely aware of who you really are but also aware that you are forgiven, accepted, loved, and redeemed. Both sinner and saint, rebel and ambassador. Both the harlot and the bride.

The sharper we see our failings, the clearer we'll see our need for a Savior and the more real his love will appear in our lives. My soul is splintered and scarred, but sacred still, and precious to God. It's a strange and terrible and lovely feeling to see both the depth of my fallenness and the height of God's forgiveness at the same time; to experience fear and joy together in one breath, in one moment.

I've learned that to understand grace, I need to see both the holiness of God and the unholiness of myself. I need to keep them both in view. To see only sin leads to despair; to see only a Savior leads to a false sense of security. But to see both leads to Christianity.

When I was researching joy for that sermon I did, I stumbled across this letter, written in the middle of the third century, about AD 250, by a man named Cyprian. Here's what he wrote to his friend Donatus:

This is a cheerful world as I see it from my garden under the shadows of my vines. But if I were to ascend some high mountain and look out over the wide lands, you know very well what I should see: brigands on the highways, pirates on the sea, armies fighting, cities burning; in the amphitheaters men murdered to please applauding crowds; selfishness and cruelty and misery and despair under all roofs. It is a bad world, Donatus, an incredibly bad world. But I have discovered in the midst of it a quiet and holy people who have learned a great secret. They have found a joy which is a thousand times better than any pleasure of our sinful life. They are despised and persecuted, but they care not. They are masters of their souls. They have overcome the world. These people, Donatus, are the Christians—and I am one of them.[1]

This man who overcame the world, St. Cyprian, was later put to death for his newfound joy and his newly embraced faith. It is a bad world after all—bloody and messy and fragile and sad. We see that for ourselves when we step out of the sheltered garden and look out over the wide lands. We hear about it when we flip on the nightly news.

But a powerful joy is available. A sacred, secret laughter rising from the throat of a slaughtered God. A joy that can crack open the deepest sadness of the world because it knows how to conquer death itself.

I too have discovered a people—pierced with truth and drenched with joy—who are able to overcome their circumstances because of a wall that surrounds their souls. They have entered the paradox of pain and joy. These people are Christians. And I am one of them.

— six

ludicrous love

The thirteenth chapter of 1 Corinthians contains one of the most famous descriptions of love ever written. I've seen it reprinted on plaques, bookmarks, Bible covers, and T-shirts. It's probably on a billboard somewhere. Maybe even on the seat of some girl's pants. I hope not, but I wouldn't doubt it.

I decided to personalize Paul's poetic treatise on love and see how I measured up:

> Steve is patient, Steve is kind. He does not envy, he does not boast, he is not proud. He is not rude, he is not self-seeking, he is not easily angered, he keeps no record of wrongs.
>
> Steve does not delight in evil but rejoices with the truth. He always protects, always trusts, always hopes, always perseveres.
>
> Steve never fails.
>
> (based on 1 Corinthians 13:4–8 NIV)

Um, okay, so that's maybe not entirely, *100 percent* accurate. I have a feeling the following wording is a little more on target:

Steve is impatient and sometimes mean. He envies other people (especially authors who sell more books than he does), he pretends to be humble, he is proud. He is all too often rude; he is self-seeking, easily angered, and keeps track of wrongs.

Steve frequently delights in evil (although it's hard for him to admit it) yet rejoices with the truth when it benefits him. He sometimes protects, occasionally trusts, and hopes to persevere.

Steve often fails.

(based on reality)

In the nineteenth-century Christian classics *The Way of a Pilgrim* and *Pilgrim Continues His Way*, an anonymous Christian tells of his travels throughout Russia seeking people who can teach him how to pray without ceasing. Eventually he meets a priest who tells him his biggest problem is that he doesn't love God, that he hates his neighbors, that he doesn't really believe God's words, and that he's filled with pride. This is quite a shock to the pilgrim. Then the priest hands him a document entitled "A Confession Which Leads the Inward Man to Humility." What struck me most as I read the document was the section on how we don't really love our neighbors:

> If I did love him as myself, as the gospel bids, his misfortunes would distress me also, his happiness would bring delight to me too. But, on the contrary, I listen to curious, unhappy stories about my neighbor, and I am not distressed; I remain quite undisturbed or, what is still worse, I find a sort of pleasure in them. . . . His well-being, honor, and happiness do not delight me as my own, and, as if they were something quite alien to me, give me no feeling of gladness. What is more, they subtly arouse in me feelings of envy or contempt.[1]

After reading the priest's document, the pilgrim becomes horrified. "Good heavens! What frightful sins there are hidden within me, and up to now I've never noticed them!"[2]

When I read *Pilgrim Continues His Way* I realized I have a lot to learn about love. Just like that stunned pilgrim, my love tends to be sporadic, hesitant, and often just a form of selfishness in disguise. Sometimes I think I know how to love others, but at times I wonder if I love, truly love, anything other than myself. I can identify with that pilgrim: this realization can be horrifying indeed.

In Psalm 13:5, King David referred to God's love as "unfailing."

I can tell I'm not God because when I look at my life, all I see is failing love. In my failing love, I forget to get a birthday present for my brother, but I remember the last time he insulted me. In my failing love, I tell my wife how much I adore her, and then I step on her feelings when the wash isn't folded and the checkbook isn't in that little plastic holder thing on our kitchen table where it is Supposed To Be All The Time. In my failing love, I talk about giving God my all but end up giving him my leftovers.

In my failing love, I say things I know I'll regret even as I say them and leave unsaid the words that might have actually done some good if only I'd had the courage to speak up. I find it easier to be impatient than reasonable, resentful than forgiving, and critical than kind. And when it comes to living sacrificially for others, most of the time I'd rather not go there. Typically, I only make sacrifices for myself.

"I hate it," a friend of mine told me once. "I hurt most those closest to me, and I can't seem to stop." I wasn't sure what to say. I'd seen him lose his cool with his kids; I'd heard the way he talked to his wife. He'd even lashed out at me a few times. But I didn't feel qualified to give him a whole lot of advice in the matter, because I've done the same things.

If only I could learn to treat my family with the same courtesies I give to strangers at the supermarket. St. John pointed out that anyone who lives only for himself is still dead: "A person who has no love is still dead" (1 John 3:14). Sometimes I wonder if I'm still dead in the ways that matter most.

In my failing love, I see the faults of other people spread out before me all the way to the horizon but don't tend to notice anything at all wrong with my own life, priorities, or attitude. I can't seem to find my own faults even when I pick through my heart with tweezers.

I've taken failed love to an entirely new level.

That's how little I understand love.

So when I experience unfailing love, it astounds me. I see glimpses of this kind of love sometimes. In smiles and tears and hugs and restored relationships. In people who accept me despite how flawed and imperfect and blunt and moody I can be. Just these glimpses can be life transforming.

I was at a retreat one time, and a friend of mine from Canada danced a prayer to Jesus. I felt so awkward watching her that I had to close my eyes. Not because of the way she danced, like it was erotic or something, but because of the passion that flowed through her to the Almighty. I felt like I was intruding on her prayer, like it was spiritual voyeurism to watch her reveal her soul like that to the Lord. Her whole body flowed with unbridled love for God. It was awe inspiring. It made me think of what love would look like with feet.

Sometimes true love looks like a mother nursing her baby, or a father playing Chutes and Ladders with his son, or a woman dancing with her eyes closed before the Lord.

> ah, what wonderful listening it takes
>   to hear
> a heartbeat across the room.
>
> ah, what magnificent vision it takes
>   to see
> a broken heart.
>
> but how rare it is to see with those eyes
>   and to hear with such finely attuned ears.

And then, of course, there's God and his perfect, unfailing, unfaltering, everlasting love. As one of my sisters in the faith once told me, "The one who knows you best loves you most." He knows who I am, and he loves me with his scarred, sacrificial, ludicrous brand of love.

Could it really be true that I am infinitely more precious to him than he is to me? That I'm accepted even though I'm unacceptable? That I'm loved even though I'm unlovable? That in him my soul can find its true worth, even though I am, on my own, unworthy? I can hardly grasp these things.

Jesus offers incomprehensible love to his followers every day. His love didn't fail when his disciples ran off but sought them out in the upper room after his rising from the dead. His love didn't fail when the soldiers nailed him to the cross but found the words to pray for their forgiveness. His steady, unflinching love led him to the cross, through the grave, and then back to this side of eternity to reassure his followers of God's preposterous passion for us. His love didn't fail when he found me wandering through the wilderness of life as a college senior, and it hasn't yet let me go.

I look across my life and see so many storms. I look across his grace and see so many horizons.

When my middle daughter, Ariel, was still a baby and not yet fully exposed to the failing loves of this world, I wrote this poem:

my daughter lays her hand on mine.
young blood courses through her fingers
and warms the top of my hand. her fingers widen
so that she can hold on.

she flexes her fingers and there are no wrinkles
on her skin. it is as young as the dawn.
no scars mark her hand, it's as innocent as a lily.
no tales are written on her skin.
but there will be. if her hand continues to grow
and reach out for mine.

touch.

We reach out for each other; we have to, because we're human. And we hurt each other—often the ones we love the most. Because we are human.

∽

Love, just like life, always involves risk. You cannot fully, truly love someone without risking your feelings, your time, your future. Those who are afraid to risk are afraid to love, because intimacy requires risk. Until you open your heart to someone to show them where you hurt the most, you'll never find intimacy or uncover the deepest secrets of love. And until we do that with God, we don't see the true depths of his love for us.

Part of the terror of daily life is the mystery of love's unchained, unexplained power in our world. Because as we all know, the more you love, the more you'll be hurt when your lover betrays you. So when you think about it, God's heart must be the most wounded of all.

I think most of us have discovered that the more we love others, the more we're able to love them; that love given is love grown. So no matter how hard I try, I can't use up the love in my heart by giving it away. Love regenerates, multiplies exponentially whenever it's shared, so that the only way to end up with an empty, loveless heart is to horde my love, to hold it back. By keeping love inside, I kill it off. It evaporates. By offering it to others, it grows deeper roots in my soul.

In addition, the more we love, the greater our capacity to love grows. Like the widow of Zarephath's jar of oil, love given is love restored. (Okay, I know that came out of nowhere, but if you're not familiar with the story, check it out; it's a good one. You can find it in 1 Kings 17:7–24.)

In one of my old journals I found the following quote, written right after I became a believer. (I'm not sure if I made it up or copied it down from a church sign somewhere. I might actually have made it up.) Here it is: "A funny thing about Jesus is that the more he fills your heart, the roomier it becomes."

Ask any parent if they think they can use up their love for their kids by living it out day by day, and they'll give you the same answer: never.

Of course, love can be lost. I know that. I guess we all do. Love can grow cold, relationships can wither, friendships can die away. Just look at the daytime talk shows or divorce statistics and you'll see how fractured and lost and splintered our relationships can become.

Sometimes misunderstandings happen or people move away or we just lose interest in each other. But I think most of the time the withering begins when the lovers begin thinking of and living for themselves rather than the beloved. As soon as we start to expect something in return for our love, it's no longer freely given. That's why Paul could write, "Let no debt remain outstanding, except the continuing debt to love one another, for he who loves his fellowman has fulfilled the law" (Romans 13:8 NIV). Love is a debt that you willingly live with and can never repay. It makes us continually indebted to those we meet. When we expect to get paid back, we begin to lose our love. Love is the unpayable debt that fulfills God's ultimate requirements.

So here's the paradox of love: the people with the emptiest lives are those who give of themselves the least, while those with the fullest lives are the ones who are always giving themselves away. Seeing this strange aspect of love helps me to understand how Jesus is able to love each of us with perfect, unfailing love.

God gives all of himself, offers the complete package of his love, to each of us and so receives, in the act of giving, even more love to extend. And then the giving begins again. Perfect love given and received, unending sacrifice. Unfailing love.

The more richly he loves one, the more fully he can love all. God's love continually renews itself. His mercies are new every day. His grace is fresh every morning. His presence is available every moment.

By the way, I often have to remind myself of this because his love doesn't always look like I expect it to. Sometimes when I see the cir-

sailing between the stars

cumstances of my life, if I'm not careful, I'm tempted to doubt God's love rather than be comforted by it. If things go my way, I tend to think of myself as being in the grip of his love, but when life hammers me, when the Joy won't come off my pants, I start wondering what I did to really tick him off.

God's love can even come cleverly disguised as pain: "'The Lord disciplines those he loves, and he punishes those he accepts as his children.' As you endure this divine discipline, remember that God is treating you as his own children. Whoever heard of a child who was never disciplined?" (Hebrews 12:6–7). As the French priest François de Fénelon noted, "The more God loves you, the less He spares you."[3]

Well then, honestly, there are times I wish God didn't love me so much. I wish he'd spare me some of his painful love. I'd rather be spoiled once in a while instead of disciplined so much; maybe he could be more like a grandpa visiting for the weekend and less like a dad doing his best to raise a resilient, self-confident child in a world of methamphetamines, date rape, and puberty.

> you don't hold my past before me to accuse me.
>   you hold your story before me to pardon me.
> you love me with an extravagance i cannot understand.
> majesty circles out from your heart
> and dives deeply into the soul of my surrender.
> all of life is your gift to me.
> even when your love tastes like pain
> to my earth-nurtured tongue.

I heard a story about a man who walked twelve miles to give a missionary a hand-woven basket he'd made him for Christmas. The missionary was thankful for the gift but asked the guy, "Why did you bring this to me today? I'll be visiting your village next week."

"This is the day we celebrate the birth of the Master, not next week."

"Yes," said the missionary, "I know. But I just wish you wouldn't have had to walk so far."

And the man replied, "The walk was part of the gift."

John 3:16, perhaps the most famous New Testament verse of all, says, "For God so loved the world that he gave his only Son, so that everyone who believes in him will not perish but have eternal life." Often Christians use this verse to bring to mind the death of Jesus, but Jesus was the one who said it, so I think he's talking about his life, not just his death. After all, God didn't kill Jesus; we were the ones who did that. His Father didn't just send Jesus to die for us; he sent him to live for us.

The long walk through this life was part of the gift. Every breath Jesus breathed was part of the gift. Every board he sawed, every story he told, every scar he bore was part of the life he lived for me. And his death and his rising were part of the long walk too. That's what love looks like. That's a love that doesn't fail.

His is an exquisite and incomprehensible love. A love I will never understand, yet a love I cannot imagine living without. God is actually fond of me. From before time began, there has never been a single moment when I haven't been at the forefront of his thoughts and the center of his heart.

I can hardly believe it. He would rather die than live for an eternity in paradise without me by his side. I am actually more important to God than life itself.

I know this kind of love doesn't make sense. If God acted according to logic, he would always bless the faithful and punish the wicked. Sure, then he would make perfect sense, but his Son never would have volunteered for the cross. And he never would have started the long walk to my heart.

So here's one final version of 1 Corinthians 13. God is love and Jesus is God, so let's try it like this:

Jesus is patient, Jesus is kind. He does not envy, he does not boast, he is not proud. He is not rude, he is not self-seeking, he is not easily angered, he keeps no record of wrongs.

Jesus does not delight in evil but rejoices with the truth. He always protects, always trusts, always hopes, always perseveres.

Jesus never fails.

There. That's better. That version actually sounds right.

— seven

fleshing out jesus

Although He is God and man, He is not two, but one Christ.
And He is one, not because His divinity was changed into flesh, but
   because His humanity was assumed unto God.
He is one, not by a mingling of substances, but by unity of person.

The Athanasian Creed

I'm ashamed to admit it, but at times I've acted very much like those explanatory preachers who summarize everything with little blanks and acronyms and clever alliteration. They can take any Bible story or poem and distill it down into its three essential points that all happen to begin with the same letter. It's an amazing skill. During their sermons, I always try to guess what'll fit in the next blank. Sometimes it keeps me occupied the whole service.

And even though that approach seems to work for some people, it always diminishes the stories for me. The more I can explain a story, the less interested in it I become. Stories become less substantial and less transformative when I can tie them up with a tidy little bow of explanation, because the things I can define no longer intrigue me. It's usually those stories that I can't quite wrap my arms around that grab hold of me and won't let me go. Sometimes forever.

So these days when I read Bible stories, I don't look for the lesson or the main point or the key verse so much anymore. Instead, I look for the struggle, for what doesn't fit, for what goes wrong, for the things that truly set the story into motion. This approach has really changed the way I understand the story God is telling our world.

For example, I always used to think the account of Jesus being left behind in Jerusalem when he was a boy was about how Mary and Joseph lost him and then finally found him at the temple (see Luke 2:41–52). It seems pretty straightforward.

But then I started looking for the struggle, for the heartbeat of the tale, and I realized this story is about something else entirely. Something I'd always managed to miss.

Here's the story: every year Mary and Joseph took Jesus to the Passover festival in Jerusalem. Then the year Jesus turned twelve, they accidentally left him behind when they started on their trip back home to Nazareth. At first they thought maybe Jesus was with some of their friends or relatives in the caravan, but when he didn't show up, they got worried and began to look for him.

Still unsuccessful, they returned to Jerusalem and spent several days in a frantic search, until at last they found him conversing with the religious scholars at the temple. Mary was exasperated. "Son!" she cried. "Why have you done this to us? Your father and I have been frantic, searching for you everywhere" (Luke 2:48). But Jesus replied, "Why did you need to search? . . . You should have known that I would be in my Father's house" (Luke 2:49).

Luke closes the story by noting that neither Mary nor Joseph had any idea what Jesus was talking about, but Jesus returned with them and was obedient to them, and his mother "stored all these things in her heart" (Luke 2:51).

That's the *Reader's Digest* condensed version. Now, here's what I see going on.

Almost always, the person who struggles with something and then discovers something is the main character of a story. I used to think this story was about Jesus, but then I noticed that he doesn't really struggle with anything. He always knows what he's doing, where he is, and why he's there. That leaves his mom and his foster dad, Joseph, as possible main characters. And since Joseph has no lines in this story, I believe this is mainly a story about Mary. Already that's different than what I learned in Sunday school.

Most of the best stories have both an external struggle (a problem that needs to be solved) and an internal struggle (a question that needs to be answered). You see it in movies and novels all the time. As the FBI agent defuses the bomb, he realizes how fragile life is and decides to reconcile with his dying father, whom he hasn't spoken with since his divorce ten years earlier. Or as Brenda finally lands the job she's been trying desperately to get, suddenly it dawns on her that she really *is* in love with Edwin, who is about to move to Wichita because he thinks she's actually in love with Brent, the vacuum cleaner salesman. . . . You get the picture. External and internal struggles play off each other to add tension and depth to stories.

This story of the mother of a prepubescent deity is no different. Her external struggle is pretty clear—she can't find her son. But what about an internal struggle? Is there a question she needs answered?

I think there is. And I think she reveals it in the words she says to Jesus: "Son! . . . Why have you done this to us? Your father and I have been frantic, searching for you everywhere!" (Luke 2:48). She meant, of course, that she and Joseph had been searching for Jesus. But in truth Jesus's real Father hadn't been looking for him at all. Mary should have remembered her encounter with the angel and the miraculous, Spirit-induced conception of her boy. According to the Gospel writers, God himself, in a mystical and mysterious way, was Jesus's Father. So when Mary said, "Your dad and I have been looking all over for you!" she showed her inner struggle—she'd started to think of Joseph as her son's dad. She'd forgotten who Jesus really was and why he'd come to earth in the first place.

And by his reply, Jesus put a magnifying glass up to her struggle. "Why did you need to search? . . . You should have known that I would be in my Father's house" (Luke 2:49). He could have said, "You should have known that I'd be in the temple" or "back here in Jerusalem" or "learning about God" or something like that. But he didn't. He said "in my Father's house." And I don't believe it was a coincidence. Jesus always chose his words carefully.

Mary forgot.

He was so normal, so human, so much like everyone else that I think she forgot about his divine lineage and his ultimate purpose in life. She forgot he was God. If she had remembered his true identity, she would have known immediately where to look for him. And she never would have referred to her husband as Jesus's dad.

(By the way, where's Joseph through all this? Well, quiet. In the background. Just taking it all in. I think he was a man of few words. As my pastor pointed out to me, "None of his words are recorded in the Bible. Anywhere. Typical guy.")

So now does Mary's life change as a result of this encounter? I'd say so. She pondered the events in her heart, and through the rest of the Bible we never hear her referring to Joseph as Jesus's father again. Ever.

Struggle. Discovery. Change.

The more I explored this story, the more I realized it really isn't about Jesus being lost—he wasn't lost at all. It's a story about *Mary* being lost. He stayed behind in Jerusalem on purpose because his mom had gotten used to having him around. The mystery of his true identity had faded with the years as his baby teeth fell out and his voice began to change and his acne started flaring up. Just like any other boy. He was just so human she forgot who he really was.

So he stayed behind to remind her.

And me.

> mary's womb
> whispered forth
> the talking tale.
>> on that starry night
>> in a gush of blood,
>>> the story was finally born.
> and when they cut the cord
> to free him from his mother
> he wailed out the first note
> of this fabulous fable called
>> *life*.

∽

Most paintings and statues of Jesus make me feel sorry for him. He has this spaced-out look on his face like he's either on drugs or has just finished watching C-SPAN for eight hours straight. His head is tilted to the side. His eyes peer entreatingly toward heaven. He's limp and pale and emaciated. He doesn't look anything like a battle-scarred serpent slayer. More like a nurse's aide or something.

When it comes to caricatures of God, the limp little Jesus is one of the cruelest ones I can imagine, because it makes me feel sorry for him rather than drop to my knees in awe of him. It doesn't look anything like the thundering, rage-filled carpenter who drove crooks out of the temple with a whip he made himself. By hand. It doesn't bring to mind the powerful voice of truth that silenced the sea with a single word and leveled a mob of angry soldiers with one simple question. It doesn't show me the man who, without flinching, faced a rioting mob of villagers armed with rocks.

The limp little Jesus would have cowered in a corner, but the Carpenter of Time stared them down and walked right through their midst to go get himself some supper.

Religion and tradition have made it harder than ever to crack through the crust of our preconceptions and uncover the nourishing, disturbing truth of who Jesus really is.

And it isn't skeptics who have done this. Sadly, so much of the real Jesus has been sanitized and neutered over the years by well-meaning church people. I think they feel a need to protect him, but you don't protect your sword; you use it to fight with. You don't need to protect Jesus—he's the first and last weapon in God's quiver.

Here is a man full of furious love. Here is a man whose blood is on fire. Hurricanes and demons step aside to let him pass. Anytime we picture him as weak or helpless or pathetic, we're only holding a mirror up to our own souls because this skin-covered God is mightier than the stars.

I love how Kahlil Gibran described Jesus in the essay he wrote on Good Friday called "The Crucified":

> Jesus was not a bird with broken wings; He was a raging tempest who broke all crooked wings. . . . Free and brave and daring He was. He defied all despots and oppressors. . . . He did not persuade the strong man to become a monk or a priest, but He came to send forth upon this earth a new spirit, with power to crumble the foundation of any monarchy built upon human bones and skulls.[1]

Jesus is not a bird with broken wings. He is not limp. And he is not weak. He is the passionate fury and the furious passion of the infinite and almighty God.

And yet . . . he was meek enough to wash the feet of his followers, humble enough to be laid in a manger, playful enough to let kids tug at his beard, and tolerant enough to party with prostitutes.

Yes, he was the baby in the manger. Yes, he is the man who made demons tremble. Yes, he is the Lamb of God. Yes, he is the Lion of Thunder. Here is a man who is not ashamed to weep in front of the crowds, and neither is he afraid to accuse—to their faces—the most powerful men in the land of spiritually abusing the people.

He is both. He is all. The beginning and the end. The author and the ink. Love piercing time. Mystery living next door.

A few years ago I wrote a children's book called *Believe It: Bible Basics That Won't Break Your Brain*. I tried to convey the enigma of Jesus's birth in a way kids could understand. Here's what I wrote:

> The Word poured himself into a baby so small.
> He was born in a stable and slept in a stall.
> He was God wrapped in man like words wrapped in a song
> So helplessly human, yet all-mightily strong!
> (And pleasing to God 'cause he never did wrong.)
> Not just God, not just Man, not just one or the other,
> But both man and God! Both our Savior and brother!
> Both human and holy, a guy and a God!
> How strange! How amazing! How unusually odd!
> (I'm glad he was human and not tuna or cod.)[2]

Jesus is the umbilical cord to the real, the bridge between the finite and the infinite, and the lifeline between a lost and lonely race and our patient, searching God. Here is the Creator of the cosmos growing slowly in the womb of his mother. Here is a man with the meekness of a little girl in ponytails and the strength of a Titan crushing a mountain.

Over the years, as they've attempted to make sense of the world, some people have tried to differentiate the sacred from the secular, but here in this God-Man, that division is erased forever. In fact, Paul calls Christ's divine humanity the central mystery of Christianity: "Without question, this is the great mystery of our faith: Christ appeared in the flesh and was shown to be righteous by the Spirit" (1 Timothy 3:16).

Jesus, the one whom the heavens cannot contain, fit inside a manger. On a starry night in a sleepy town, the eternal one was born. And that night the one who never slumbers nor sleeps, the King of All the Galaxies, dozed just a few feet away from a donkey's butt.

Absurd? Absolutely.

Preposterous? Duh.

True? Well, yeah, actually it is.

> cell by cell, woven and
> grown. deity and humanity both
> dwell in the heart
> of my precious, helpless,
> thunderous, embryonic God.
> your birth brought labor pains
> to the world and the final
> inception of blood-washed joy.

Personally, I don't have too much trouble picturing Jesus as either a man or a God—one or the other. I can accept that he was a person like me who got frustrated, annoyed, exasperated, angry, depressed, and tired after a hard day's work. Or I can see him as a deity raising the dead, healing the sick, or controlling the weather. But what I just can't wrap my mind around is that he is both as human as I am and as different from me as God is. Totally human. Totally holy. A guy and a God.

The lion and the lamb are one. Yet he's not half-lion and half-lamb. The king of the universe is the servant of all. Yet he's not half-king and half-servant. He's completely both. Fully mystery and fully truth. Fully God and fully man. Eternal, and yet able to lay down his life. All-knowing, and yet perplexed by the unbelief of his hometown's skeptics.

A dying deity.

God with nostrils.

Just like everyone else, Jesus ate, slept, laughed, and peed. Sometimes he got angry. Sometimes he was sad. He cracked his back and pulled a muscle now and then and stubbed his toes and occasionally got food stuck in his teeth. He had headaches and heartaches and crushes. He knew what it was like to sweat and hope and wonder and question and deal with temptation.

And suffering. He knew about that too.

He was as real as a sunny day.

How could it be? How could he be the eternal, infinite, immortal, and unchangeable God and at the same time be a helpless baby pooping in his swaddling clothes?

Don't ask me to explain it. I can't.

In a certain way, everyone is fully at least two things at the same time without mixing the nature of those two things. I'm fully a son and fully a father, not half of each. I'm fully body and fully soul, not half one and half the other. But with Jesus we're talking about being fully God and fully human. That's the kicker.

It's fascinating to me that those who knew Jesus firsthand never tried to explain *how* he could be God enmeshed in flesh. Instead, they wrote just as naturally about his deity as they did about his humanity. Here's how Jesus's friend John described the paradox of his buddy's true identity: "He was in the world, and though the world was made through him, the world did not recognize him. . . . The Word became flesh and made his dwelling among us" (John 1:10, 14 NIV).

If you think about it, Jesus couldn't really be *either* a man or a God. It doesn't make sense for him to be one or the other. A mere man couldn't have done the miracles he did and wouldn't have made the outrageous claims he did—that he and God are one, that no one can come to God

sailing between the stars

except through him, that he himself is the resurrection and the life we need, that without him we have no hope, and that coming to him is our only chance of obtaining heaven, finding peace with God, or receiving eternal life.

And conversely, a God wouldn't have met with the failures and resistance that he did. After all, Jesus admitted he didn't know everything, he couldn't do miracles in his hometown among the scoffers who doubted his claims, and in the end, he died. How could God do that?

Maybe he's neither a man nor a God. He could be an alien, maybe. Or a time traveler from the future with a bag full of tricks and cool science experiments that looked like miracles to first-century fishermen. I guess you can believe whatever you want to about him. But if you take him at his word, he was both the Son of Man and the Son of God.

One of my favorite descriptions of a good story comes from novelist Flannery O'Connor: "When you can state the theme of a story, when you can separate it from the story itself, then you can be sure the story is not a very good one. The meaning of a story has to be embodied in it, has to be made concrete in it. A story is a way to say something that can't be said any other way, and it takes every word in the story to say what the meaning is."[3]

Well, Jesus is a story that cannot be summarized, prodded at, or explained. He's the ultimate meaning of the tale God is telling our planet. He is the Word of God embedded and embodied in the human race. His life is a way of saying something that couldn't be said any other way, and it takes every word in the Story to say what the meaning is.

Mary forgot this. And I do too.

∿

I'll admit that part of me is a little annoyed by the fact that I can't understand Jesus. I sort of wish I could hold on to all aspects of him at once.

But then again, I guess I'm glad there's a mysterious, incomprehensible aspect to him. I wouldn't want to worship a God who could fit inside my explanations. After all, faith is the ability to see truth that's invisible; it's not the ability to comprehend the incomprehensible.

Jesus is the breath I breathe in the moments when I am finally alive, the fire I touch when my heart explodes with the mysteries of faith, the laughter I hear when I close my eyes near the playground at recess. He is the hope rising in my heart as I sit on my porch in the early autumn morning and watch the mists sort their way through the oak trees in my backyard. Jesus is the marvel in my soul.

Here is the mystery of the ages with morning breath and dimples.

Here is a man able to speak the stars into existence and breathe grace into my heart.

> in your arms i am a bride
> and you are the confident groom.
> you are a whisper of hot breath
> caressing my cheek. the fingers
> of your presence cling to
> the back of my neck,
> graze across my forehead,
> encircle my heart. the gracious
> warmth of your voice chills me
> whenever i hear the deep,
> resonant silences of your love.
> passion like this cannot be
> called anything other than holy.

Muslim Sufis have a type of enigmatic story called a *koan* that has no right interpretation—you just turn it over in your head to reach new levels of enlightenment. Jesus was a living koan. Look at him from this perspective and he seems as human as you and I. But turn his life over in your head and you can't help but see diamond-quality divinity shining through the cracks.

I'm glad I don't serve a deity I can cram into my brain-sized understanding of the world. If I could, I would be more than human, and he would be less than God. Mystery always exceeds knowledge, always swirls out beyond the borders and encircles the whole. By definition God must be bigger than my knowings, or he couldn't be who he is.

The deeper I dig into Jesus, the more mystery I find. And when I finally do look for him, I discover him there in his Father's house again. Doing his Father's will. Reminding me of who he truly is and inviting me to enter the family of fools.

— eight

the crux

Rock climbers have a term for the most difficult part of the climb: the *crux*. It usually involves a combination of moves and holds that appear impossible at first. Often it's the critical point, the crucial moment in the climb.

I'm not by any stretch of the imagination an expert climber, but I love to go climbing with my friends whenever I can. And whenever I'm on a climb and I come to the crux, I always start thinking, *There's no way I can do this! I can't make it! I'm gonna peel!* And sometimes I do. I fall.

But if I make it past the crux, I can look back and finally see the route clearly. Once you're past the crux, the route up the cliff makes sense at last.

Crux is a Latin word. It means cross.

∾

I think most of us would prefer a safely packaged, hermetically sealed, tame little God. Maybe spread a little Jesus across the surface of our lives every now and then so we can remain pretty much who we are, but with a spiritual coating. Like a little strawberry cream cheese on the bagel of our souls. But Jesus shatters us the moment we try to make him reasonable. He refuses to become our pet. He must be our master or our nothing at all.

In order to tone down the wild claims of Jesus, we tend to emasculate his words. We try to move him into the middle ground of practicality, into the territory of compromise and tolerance. We want to take the edge off. Sand off the corners of his commands. Not ruffle any feathers. We want him to be a nice, inspiring, thought-provoking, soothing spiritual guide. An Oprah for our souls. But the moment we do that, his blunt words and narrative artistry shatter our misconceptions once again. He escapes every effort at categorization and caricature-ization.

> i know a carpenter who
> built a kingdom by letting
> himself get nailed to the
> wooden beams of my soul.
> and through the ages and through the questions
> no storm has ever knocked it down.
> knocked him down.
> > huh. who knew that blood would be
> > such a strong and time-resistant adhesive?

The more you get to know Jesus, the clearer and more mystifying he appears—often at the same time. As soon as I try to label him as a liberalist or a literalist, a progressive or a conservative, he splinters my stereotypes. As soon as I think I've got him pinned down, he wrestles free, and I find that I'm the one who's pinned to the mat.

"Go ahead and stone her," he says, so he must support the death penalty. He must! He's probably a right-wing fundamentalist. One of *them*.

But then he continues, "If you have no sin, throw the first stone." Oh, well, um, maybe he's for forgiveness and rehabilitation after all. Maybe he's one of those granola-eating liberals, in lockstep with the Hollywood elite. I should have guessed as much by looking at his haircut.

It's amazing that with all the scrutiny of the ages, Jesus just becomes more and more admirable. And yet more perplexing too.

Here is a man of paradox and poetry, ripe with both fury and love. And his words and teachings pulsate with a life all their own, working somehow to both comfort and confront wandering souls. And then of course you've got his stories—those unsettling parables that are able to leave fragments of light in the souls of even the most dark-hearted listeners.

This man whom the angels called "the Prince of Peace" has caused a rift in the world that cuts through cultures, traditions, countries, and families. He brings division wherever he's introduced into the conversation because he will not be ignored and he cannot be stepped over. And he brings peace because he offers God's raw, real, unvarnished love. He carries both a peace treaty from heaven and a sword of truth for slicing through rigid souls and frozen hearts.

In Jesus I find rage and forgiveness, sorrow and joy, love and truth. All of the above. Jesus is the dancing stillness of the ages. What dawn is to the night and spring is to the winter, so Jesus is to my soul.

In his teachings this enigmatic rabbi outlined a puzzling new way of life in which the most dissatisfied become the most fulfilled, insults bring blessings, the first become last, and the most humble become the most exalted.

A few years ago I went to speak at a children's camp in Texas. No one there had ever heard me speak before. When I walked in, the director looked at me skeptically. "Bubba was our camp pastor last year," she said. "Bubba juggled fire. Do you juggle fire?"

"Um, no, I don't juggle fire."

"Bubba rode a unicycle. Do you ride a unicycle?"

"No."

"Can you escape from a straightjacket?"

"I don't think so."

She looked at me disdainfully. "Then what do you *do*?"

"Well, mostly I just tell stories."

There was a long pause, and then, "Don't be surprised if a lot of people keep talking about Bubba."

If being humbled means you get to be exalted, I think right about then I was feeling like the most acclaimed guy in the galaxy. There's nothing like being caught in the middle of one of Jesus's awkward paradoxes.

∽

Any way you cut it, you can't keep Jesus at arm's length. Looking into his face is both comforting and distressing. And eventually, if you look into his true countenance long enough, you'll either lean into his embrace in surrender or turn your back on him and run for your life.

There's no middle ground here; nothing about him is reasonable. His teachings simply refuse to be diluted. At every turn Jesus draws another line in the sand. "If you're not for me, you're against me," he said. "If you're not gathering, you're scattering" (see Matthew 12:30). But my heart doesn't like having a line drawn in the sand. It prefers a big beach party where nothing much is asked of me and we can all feel good about ourselves together while we roast marshmallows in the moonlight. So I'm struck by his words—both reassured by them and deeply alarmed.

For example, Jesus once said, "Be perfect" (Matthew 5:48) and offered no disclaimers or exemptions. Modern evangelicals do, though. We're quick to explain away his words: "Oh, that's in the Sermon on the Mount. Jesus is just saying those things to show us we can never be perfect. After all, we're saved by grace."

It's funny Jesus never explained it like that. Instead he said that those who hear his words and don't put them into practice are fools and that those who claim to know him but don't obey him were never part of

God's kingdom in the first place (see Matthew 7:21–29). Heresy comes the moment we try to make his message palatable and user-friendly.

And the problem usually isn't that we can't understand him; it's simply that we don't want to obey him. As the Danish philosopher Søren Kierkegaard wrote, "The matter is quite simple. The Bible is very easy to understand. But we Christians are a bunch of scheming swindlers. We pretend to be unable to understand it because we know very well that the minute we understand we are obliged to act accordingly."[1]

Be perfect—two words that slam into me like a locomotive, leaving no wiggle room or excuses. And yet here's another of Jesus's teachings: "Come to me. I'll carry your burdens. I'll give rest to your soul" (see Matthew 11:28–29).

On the one hand he gives a command; on the other, an invitation. And even though these two teachings stand in stark contrast to each other, Jesus doesn't offer us the option of compromise to bring harmony to them. He never asks us to give up one ideal for the other, or to tone down either, but to embrace them both. The one is certain condemnation, the other complete salvation—a curse and a blessing, guilt and acquittal, shame and forgiveness, anger and love, terror and comfort, all whispered by the same man to the same people.

So what do we do with these teachings? Ignore half of them? Water them down? You can if you want to. Lots of people do. But I think he wants us to enter the mystery of faith and embrace the paradox that both ideas are true in a deeper, more real way than we could ever comprehend.

I'm glad Jesus never said, "Try your hardest to be good, and God will accept you. You're only human, after all. Just do your best. No one can fault you for that. You'll certainly get to heaven if you do that, because if there is a hell, God would only send really bad people there—people like

Hitler or Jack the Ripper—never hardworking, good-looking, church-going, civic-minded people like you."

I'm glad he didn't talk like that—ever—because then he would just disappear. History would swallow him up as quickly as it swallows us. If Jesus had talked like that, his words would carry no sting, no weight, no mystery, no power. His voice would be just one among a million others offering us practical, good-sounding, helpful advice that we all know doesn't work.

Instead, Jesus was history's highest idealist and most real realist. Both.

One of the greatest, most universally consistent failures of humankind is the attempt to reach enlightenment by trying harder. From what I've seen, most Eastern religions discovered the futility of this approach long ago, while most Western religions are based squarely and entirely upon this failing enterprise.

We tell ourselves that we're pretty good, but pretty good is just another way of saying that we're at least partly bad. That's the rub.

So we try harder to be better, or we compare ourselves with others, or we tell ourselves that we're doing pretty well and God ought to at least honor that. I heard a recent survey found that 64 percent of Americans believe they'll go to heaven and .007 percent think they'll go to hell. Wow. What a spiritual country we have . . . or maybe what a deceived population we have. One of the two.

How can we ever hope to better ourselves by appealing to ourselves? Can anything rise above itself? The stuff of our souls is not the stuff of our dreams, yet that's all we can build with if we rely upon ourselves.

But if we could be touched by the divine we could become more than even our greatest dreamers dare to believe. Then we could finally overcome our failures, not by effort from below but by grace from above. And there's the crux—we need God's help, but we dread admitting it. The one thing we all know we need is the last thing any of us are willing to request.

The idea that hope can only come from outside of myself, that grace can only be found in the arms of God, that I'm sought before I become a seeker and then loved into being a lover—these are seismic truths. And they only begin to rumble through my soul when I finally admit how hopeless I am on my own. When I finally come to the cross.

another doorway

a blood-splattered lamb lies
cooling in the corner.
drops of crimson cling
to snowy winter wool—
and the doorframe glistens
in the pooling moonlight
while egyptian mothers
shriek through
the curtain of the night.

another wood.
another lamb.
another darkened sky.
another shriek
another death
another mother's cry.

the sound of hope being born
echoes with the most troubling
and glorious music of all.

the angel of the lord has learned
the meaning of these things
he's quite experienced in matters
such as these.

When we encounter the cross, the deepest slavery of all cracks open, and freedom finally unfolds in the night.

ॐ

Even when I try my hardest to be perfect, I don't come anywhere close.

I try to be self-controlled, patient, kind, loving, and fatherly in a wise and all-knowing sort of way, and I end up kicking the tires of my car.

One day we went to the beach, and I stayed out in the sun about nine hours too long. My back was burnt to a crisp and very close to the color of Angelina Jolie's lips. So I tossed and turned all night and got up cranky and angry at 5:14 a.m. to take a shower and get on with the day, only to find that the hot water heater was broken. Water ten degrees colder than ice poured onto me. I managed not to scream. Barely.

After a four-second shower, I decided to catch up on some writing. I spent an hour editing three articles that were due that day, saved them, and as I did so they mysteriously vanished from the computer. Like magic. Black magic.

So I stomped back upstairs and my wife handed me our youngest daughter, Eden, who was six months old at the time. "Would you change her this time?" Then she turned and headed back to bed before I realized it wasn't a question.

That's when I began to mumble incoherently to myself.

And I wasn't quoting Bible verses.

We were using cloth diapers, God knows why, probably to save $.02 each time the baby pooped. So we had a diaper pail that we stuck the nasty diapers in until we could wash them. On this morning it was filled to the gills with disgustingly polluted poo water. The older two girls had now gotten up and were lurking by the doorway. Twice I told them to go to the kitchen to eat breakfast, yet they lingered. I was clenching my teeth. "Pleeeeease go into the other rooooooom."

They stayed. I think they were enjoying the show.

I leaned over to get the diaper wipes and I hit my head on the shelf, and that did it.

"Aaaaaaah!" I kicked my leg backward and hit the diaper pail, sending reeking, yellowish-brown water splashing all over my two oldest daughters. All three girls started crying and screaming. Five-year-old Trinity was yelling, "Daddy got diaper water on my face!" over and over again. "Daddy got diaper water on my face!"

So then Liesl came into the room.

That was not one of the high points of our marriage.

She inhaled through her teeth so intensely I thought she was going to create a vacuum in the bathroom and maybe permanently disrupt the space-time continuum. She took over diaper-changing without a word while I started to clean things up, penitently, on my knees.

Just another day in paradise.

Finally, when things calmed down, I apologized to everyone and life trudged on. A little later that morning I found Trinity coloring at the kitchen table. "You know what rough mornings remind me of?" she said.

"What?"

"Bricks."

"Huh?"

"You know, rough mornings like we've been having and rough days and rough evenings and rough nights like we sometimes have, they make me think of bricks because they're rough."

"Oh. And what kind of a day would you like to have?"

"Smooth."

"What's smooth and soft that you'd like to have a day like?"

"A blanket."

"A blanket instead of a brick?"

"Uh-huh." She didn't look up from her drawing. "That would be nice."

sailing between the stars

What do you say in a moment like that? There's nothing to say. No matter how hard I try, I end up with just as many brick days as blanket days. As many diaper water days as beach days. I try to be happy. I try to be good. But it's never quite enough. Forget being perfect; most of the time I'm barely bearable. It's just how life is.

Yet despite the universal failure of the pursuit of happiness, we can't seem to help but pursue it. No matter what culture or country we're from, we keep telling ourselves we can be better, we can become good enough to impress God, or the gods, or fate, or L. Ron Hubbard, or Yoda, or whatever, into accepting us. But of course that's impossible, because then Jesus comes along saying, "Be perfect." I'm not certain of this, but I think that implies not kicking a pail of diaper water over onto your children.

But he doesn't really mean it, does he? That we have to be perfect?

Well, yeah. Actually, he does.

He also says, "Come to me and I'll give you rest." And in this invitation lies a touch of the divine. There's a miracle woven into those words. Does he mean that too?

Yeah, he does. He means that too.

Jesus never allowed for negotiation: *Be pretty good. Love God the best you can.*

Nope.

Instead he says, "The most important commandment is this: 'Hear, O Israel! The Lord our God is the one and only Lord. And you must love the Lord your God with all your heart, all your soul, all your mind, and all your strength'" (Mark 12:29–30). In this call to perfect love, nothing halfhearted is allowed.

It disturbs me a little bit that Jesus never asked for or allowed for half. He never said I could bring him part of my life, or some of my dreams, or a little of my devotion, or a reasonable percentage of my time. And he didn't negotiate. "Ahh, I see. I didn't realize you are so well off. All right then, if you can't give up everything for me—and I understand, really, I do—then how about, um, 5 percent? How does that sound? Or maybe 10 percent and, say, one hour a week? Is that manageable?"

He never bartered or changed the price tag. He simply said, all or nothing, you decide. "So no one can become my disciple," he told the crowds, "without giving up everything for me" (Luke 14:33).

Here's what I tend to do: I follow God to the edge of common sense and convenience, and then, when things get a little dicey, I hesitate. As long as life seems sensible, I'm willing to plug forward, but at the point where faith really enters the picture, I tend to pull back. Yet Jesus has asked us to give up all safety nets and backup plans and live with reckless abandon and total trust.

I think God hates all that is halfhearted because when you divide the most important things in half, you don't end up with half but get the opposite instead. Halfway justice is injustice. Halfway devotion is compromise. Halfway purity is sin. Halfway holiness is ungodliness. Halfway worship is ritual. Halfway love is apathy. Halfway hope is despair. Anything that's halfhearted ends up becoming all wrong. A person cannot be somewhat pure or slightly Christian.

So he tells us to be perfect. No fine print. No disclaimers. "Love God with all of your heart, soul, mind, and strength," he says, and in this he echoes what his Father demanded of the Israelites all throughout the Old Testament: "I, the LORD, am your God. You must be holy because I am holy" (Leviticus 11:44). Holy. Perfect. Wholehearted love.

"But how?" we shout. "There's no hope in that! I can't be that pure. I can't love God that perfectly even when I try my hardest! There must be some mistake, some loophole!"

But there isn't. That's the crux.

I think Jesus knows we'll respond like that, yet he doesn't tone down his language. His words are sledgehammers to pound away at our excuses and rationalizations until he has smashed them all to dust. Because only then, when we stop looking for loopholes, will we start finding him. Only after his demands have done their work does his grace come in.

Because then, with promise after promise of love and acceptance, he builds our dreams anew from the inside out.

The only way to discover the pathway through all the paradoxes of his teachings is to remember that Jesus made it past the crux, past the cross. The believer finds harmony only in the completed work of Christ. As Siegbert W. Becker wrote about those seeking God,

> Now he needs the law to show him his wretched state, and he needs the gospel to show him the way out of his impossible situation. He needs the law to destroy his pride in his own character, achievements and works. He needs the gospel to overcome the despair which follows when he finds that he stands naked and alone before God. He needs the law to destroy his faith in himself. He needs the gospel to build his faith in God. What appears impossible to fit together on paper fits perfectly in the human heart.[2]

The crux, the cross, lies before us. And it's not only our greatest problem but the only solution for homeless souls. We come in desperation and find, there in the blood-soaked wood, a doorframe that leads at last to the final freedom through the night. To the exquisitely soft blanket that covers the roughest bricks of all.

thoughts on dung and grace

I've tried fasting a few times, and it hasn't gone all that well. My friend Chris told me that he fasted one day a week, so I figured, *If he can do it, so can I.*

The first time I tried, I made it until 3:00 in the afternoon before telling myself, *It's the thought that counts, and I don't want to be legalistic about this or anything*, and headed to Taco Bell for a late breakfast. It's funny how quickly you can argue away your spiritual disciplines when your stomach is growling and another commercial for a Baja Chicken Chalupa comes on TV.

About a month later I tried again. That was the day I accidentally slept in. Halfway through the morning I realized I'd missed breakfast, so I figured I had a head start and thought maybe I could make it until the next morning—I know, I know, so very spiritual of me.

I made it until suppertime. I felt a little better about that one but still like a second-string saint. I lost two pounds, though, so that was good.

The next time I actually did make it twenty-four hours. I'm not sure if I felt closer to Jesus when I was done. Closer to anorexia, maybe, but not necessarily enlightenment.

I don't fast from food too much anymore, but about every year or so I fast from coffee for a few weeks. For a writer, that's a lot worse. Starving to death seems pretty tame compared to going a day without eight to ten cups of the elixir of paradise.

The truth is, almost everything I do for God ends up like my fasting—infused with misplaced priorities and glaring failings. The idea of fasting is that you remove something you enjoy to remind yourself that you enjoy some*one* even more. Technically I don't think you're supposed to do it just because your friend did, or because you slept in, or to lose weight, or because you don't want to be so addicted to caffeine anymore. I'd have to look it up, but I don't think any of these are the reasons given in Scripture.

Once when I was feeling weighed down by my failures, I prayed this:

> o alchemist of the ages,
> my heart is lead again.
> touch it with your spells,
> caress it with your magic,
> turn my soul golden
> with your charms.

Sometimes when I look at my life, I think I'm an awful lot like a kindergartener with a box of crayons. "Look what I drew for you, Mommy!"

"Oh, it's *beautiful*!" And she sticks it on the fridge even though she has no idea if the green lump in the middle of the page is supposed to be a gigantic frog from outer space or a seasick hippopotamus. "Absolutely beautiful!"

I bring God my fasts and my loves and my life. "Look what I drew for you, Dad!"

"Oh, it's beautiful!" he says. And despite the fact that I've scribbled so far outside the lines that it's hard to tell what in the world my life is even supposed to resemble, he accepts it and sticks it on his fridge for all the angels to see. "Look what my son drew for me today! Absolutely *beautiful!*"

∾

In the fifth chapter of 1 John, one of Jesus's closest friends makes the ludicrous claim that "everyone born of God overcomes the world" (1 John 5:4 NIV).

Now, I think I understand where he's coming from, but the problem is, most of the time I don't feel like an overcomer; I feel like the overcome. Sometimes I'm overcome by impatience or anger or greed, sometimes by prejudice or pride. Sometimes all it takes is a taco commercial to do me in.

"You are salt and light," says Jesus.

Well, most of the time I don't feel very salty or shiny. Especially when I see how far outside of the lines my choices have taken me.

It strikes me that John didn't write, "Everyone *who tries really hard* overcomes the world." Or, "Everyone who *feels like an overcomer* overcomes the world." Or, "Everyone who *has high self-esteem* overcomes the world." Instead he wrote, "Everyone born of God overcomes the world." And in the first verse of that chapter he explains how that birth happens: "Everyone who believes that Jesus is the Christ is a child of God" (1 John 5:1).

So the overcoming he's talking about isn't based on effort or feelings or self-love but on faith. As overcome as I feel, as conquering as my circumstances seem to be, my faith is the assurance that I'll come out okay in the end.

Here is the stunning promise of grace: I have already overcome life; I am already at home with God in heaven. "He raised us from the dead along with Christ," wrote Paul, "and we are seated with him in the heavenly realms—all because we are one with Christ Jesus" (Ephesians 2:6). Now, I'll admit that it doesn't seem like I'm there yet, especially when I wake up in the morning and have to pick those annoying eye crusties out of my eye sockets before I can even stumble my way to the shower, but according to St. Paul, I am actually seated with Jesus in heaven.

Though my fasts overcame me, my faith overcomes my failed fasts. So as often as I'm overcome, as much as I fail, my faith overcomes my failure to overcome.

Whew. I'll need to chew on all that for a while.

It's as if God is telling us, "You'll feel overcome sometimes, but your new identity cannot be overcome. Ever. You are no longer who you were, but you're not yet who you are, either. One day this will all be made clear; until then walk in step with my Spirit and let my grace be the centerpiece of your life."

My adopted hometown of Johnson City, Tennessee, lies nestled in a valley at the base of the Blue Ridge Mountains. Buffalo Mountain lies on the edge of town, and I go hiking up there sometimes. In the autumn, fog often crawls into the valley, enshrouding everything down below. But from up in the mountains, you can see over the fog. Once you get above the clouds, you can see the big picture. It's a lot easier to see the footwork of the day unfolding from there.

Jesus didn't feel like an overcomer when he was dying on the cross. I know that because he yelled, "My God, my God, why have you forsaken me?" (Matthew 27:46), and no one who feels like Superman yells words like those. You only yell stuff like that when you feel overcome. But even then—as overcome as Jesus felt—he was overcoming death itself. As he told his disciples, "Here on earth you will have many trials and sorrows. But take heart, because I have overcome the world" (John 16:33).

The day is much clearer than the fog makes it appear.

∽

I admit there's something attractive about ancient forms of worship, but what bothers me is when a worship service becomes dusty and duty-worn rather than vibrant and soul-shaking. It makes me think: *convalescent care for God*. I usually don't go back to churches like that. After all, the gospel should be our life support. It's supposed to keep us alive, not the other way around.

God's grace is never boring, never tired, never worn out. It's like an ever-blooming flower marking the presence of a new season in the soul. Grace is the tale that is ancient but never old, timeless but never out of date.

> the past wants to slip its
> noose around my neck,
> but grace unlocks my cell
> and leads me into the sunlight
> of a new day through the gate of
> forgiveness.

Fasting certainly has its place. So do tithing and prayer and contemplation and all the rest of the practices of the church—as long as we don't start to rely on them to do anything other than show us our need for Jesus. They're road signs; he is always the destination.

"The law was given through Moses," wrote John, "God's unfailing love and faithfulness came through Jesus Christ" (John 1:17). Some Bible translations translate "unfailing love and faithfulness" as "grace and truth." Any of the four sound good to me. Jesus came to bring us unfailing love, grace, truth, and the faithfulness of God. He didn't come to bring guilt trips, shame, regrets, worry, or fear. He didn't need to. That stuff was already here, in great big, rotting, stinking heaps.

By the way, the central purpose of God's laws was never to give us a way to work our way to heaven. Instead, they're here to wake us up and show us our need for Jesus: "God's law was given so that all people could see how sinful they were" (Romans 5:20). When guilt leads you closer to Jesus, it has served its purpose. When it leads you deeper into shame or despair, it hasn't. His laws are the lines on the coloring page. His grace is the fridge.

∾

A few years ago a friend of mine gave me his minivan.

He knew that my wife and I didn't have much money, that we were struggling to make ends meet, and that we had a growing family, so he prayed about it and thought God wanted him to give us his minivan. So he did.

At first, when he offered, I was hesitant. "How much do you want for it?"

"Nothing. I'm giving it to you."

"Um, well, I'll give you as much as I can for it."

"I don't want anything."

"A couple thousand dollars at least."

"No."

"But then I'll always feel like I owe you something. C'mon, I'll feel better if I can at least pay you—"

"I don't want you to feel better. I want you to say thank you."

I swallowed hard. "Thank you."

"You're welcome."

There's nothing more annoying than grace.

∾

God's gracious, undeserved love is a flower and a tornado, meeting and growing together into a poem. It's the lingering perfume of the holy in the path of our everyday lives. It's a sacrifice so alarming that it has driven murderers to become saints and helped a handful of loudmouthed fishermen transform the Roman Empire.

And grace is dynamic and dramatic, never static. Never boring. The last thing grace could ever be is boring. The story of Jesus is deeply shocking and disturbing and empowering. And yes, amazing too. But the moment it seems trite or boring, we've lost sight of it and have started studying history or religion or theology instead of encountering Jesus.

No one who heard him speak was ever bored. I think that's because we only enter God's kingdom when we're stirred, moved, shaken, convicted, and then comforted by the King, not bored out of our wits with our lame caricatures of God. So Jesus told stories that disturbed people enough to actually wake them up.

Grace is really hard for me to understand.

After all, it's not the same thing as lowering your expectations, and it's never an excuse that you can look forward to using after you've blown it, like the "I know God doesn't want me to do this but he'll just forgive me in the end anyway" sort of thing. The resilience of God's love is not an excuse to set about purposely breaking his heart.

When the Bible talks about grace, it's always side by side with obedience. Read 1 John 5 for yourself. You'll see promise after promise of God's acceptance and love. And then you come to the last verse, which sticks out like a fifth leg on a cow: "Dear children, keep away from anything that might take God's place in your hearts" (1 John 5:21). After all those assurances of being an overcomer, John closes by saying, "Now, don't be overcome."

This is the strange irony of grace: wherever the tale takes me, I will be loved, but I still need to keep myself from those things that lure my soul away from God.

When we follow Jesus, he doesn't let us bring along any bread crumbs to mark the trail back to our old lives. He doesn't even want us to glance back over our shoulders at the way things were. Of all the teachings of the church, this daily doctrine of obedience is the hardest to believe because it isn't understood with the mind but is borne out with the sweat and flesh and tongue of daily living.

when i walk in the ways of the night
i breathe in gasps of ragged
darkness that throw tendrils,
　　lethal and deep,
　　　down into my soul.
but when i step into the melody of dawn,
i start to glow. and the shadows
inside of me begin to recede.
　　at last.

Part of the struggle of being a believer is living in the grip of this strange thing called grace but never taking advantage of it as a free license to dishonor the King or using it as a cheap salve when our hearts are caught up in willing rebellion. Because grace is costly. Sure, we don't have to pay for the minivan, but someone does. We don't have to die on the cross. But someone did.

❦

When you've been given a gift that you didn't earn and could never afford and there's nothing you can do now or in the future to pay it back, it can be pretty unsettling. It changes you. It has to, or you didn't realize how undeserving you really were.

I think God's love is meant to be encountered, received, embraced, even guzzled and gobbled by famished souls, but not necessarily understood. If I can understand his love, then I'm looking at either a caricature of him or a caricature of myself. If God's love makes sense to me, then either I don't really understand who he is or I haven't yet come to grips with who I am. In one of his sermons my pastor read this quote from the Puritans: "You cannot think highly of yourself and God at the same time."

My daughters are very concerned about things being fair. If I buy the oldest one a piece of candy at the gas station on the way to Grandma's house, the other two girls will beg for one too. "It's not fair, Daddy!" they whine.

Here's what's at the heart of grace: God isn't being fair, but not in the way we assume. It's not that he's holding out on us; it's that he *isn't*. At all. Everyone is offered more candy than they could ever eat. He's offering us more than we deserve, and there's nothing we can do to earn it or pay him back or merit his favor in any way. Period. All we can do is believe, and even *that* is his idea.

"How much do you want for it?"

"Nothing. I'm giving it to you."

"But then I'll always feel like I owe you something. C'mon, I'll feel better if I can at least pay you—"

"I don't want you to feel better. I just want you to say thank you."

I find it significant that Jesus so often compares the spiritual life to trees, fruit, orchards, and fields. After all, he wasn't a farmer. He was a carpenter. He knew all about blueprints and building codes and work crews and construction projects, yet he rarely referred to that stuff. He never said anything like, "Being close to God is like building a house! You hammer away in the sun and the rain and the wind. It takes dedication and commitment! It takes perseverance and self-control! But you put in your time and your hard work and then, after many days, you realize you're done. You've entered the kingdom!"

I'd feel a lot more comfortable if the spiritual life were like that, if it depended on hard work and good deeds and regular progress reports. But instead, Jesus talks about bearing fruit (for a sample, read John 15:1–6). And the frustrating thing for me is that vines and trees don't *try* to bear fruit. They just do it. They just grow it. Naturally. They can't help it. It has a lot less to do with their willpower and self-control and sincerity than it does with them being planted in the right environment and nurtured with the right mixture of sunlight and soil and moisture and magic.

In one of his most unusual stories, the one I call the Parable of Poop, Jesus used the example of a tree that wouldn't produce fruit. "Cut it down," said the orchard owner. But the gardener begged for one more chance to help the tree grow. I love how the King James Version translates it: "And he answering said unto him, Lord, let it alone this year also, till I shall dig about it, and dung it: And if it bear fruit, well: and if not, then after that thou shalt cut it down" (Luke 13:8–9 KJV).

I love that it says, "I shall dig about it, and dung it." The modern translations say "fertilize it," which isn't nearly as literal or remotely as much fun to teach your kids to memorize and then recite to the other children at Sunday school.

"Give the tree one more chance," the gardener pleads. "Pour some manure on it, and let's see how it does." The growth and fruit have more to do with the right amount of digging and dung than effort on the part of the tree. Realizing something like that will really do a number on your spiritual ego. Sometimes I just need to stop trying so hard and let God dig me up and dung me for a while. Maybe I need to pray more prayers like this: "God, I know I haven't been producing much fruit lately. Forgive me for that. Please give me another chance. Dung me for a while and see how I do."

The spiritual life is an organic process that occurs naturally despite the fact that we can't nail down exactly how or when. And branches only grow if they're still attached to the vine. Jesus even went so far as to say "apart from me you can do nothing" (John 15:5). There's another blow to my spiritual self-esteem. Jesus never once said to try harder. But he did say:

> Here is another illustration of what the Kingdom of God is like: A farmer planted seeds in a field, and then he went on with his other activities. As the days went by, the seeds sprouted and grew without the farmer's help, because the earth produces crops on its own. First a leaf blade pushes

through, then the heads of wheat are formed, and finally the grain ripens. And as soon as the grain is ready, the farmer comes and harvests it with a sickle.

Mark 4:26–29

We root ourselves in the word, live simply and humbly, surround ourselves with the atmosphere of God's presence, and only then does the magic happen and fruit appear—yet even the submission and obedience that help fertilize our hearts come from faith (see Romans 1:5).

Paul wrote, "Let your roots grow down into him and draw up nourishment from him, so you will grow in faith, strong and vigorous in the truth you were taught. Let your lives overflow with thanksgiving for all he has done" (Colossians 2:7).

Despite our failures, we are loved. Despite our issues and hang-ups and mistakes, we are accepted. Despite all of our distorted motives and failed fasts and sloppily drawn choices, God still puts our pictures on his fridge. Despite how overcome the children of God feel, we have already overcome the world because he overcame the world. Sometimes the most glorious picture of God isn't a man on a cross but a weather-beaten gardener with dirt beneath his fingernails, lovingly digging around my trunk and packing in a little more dung down there by the roots.

There's nothing more annoying, and more amazing, than grace.

— ten

my biggest fan

Sometimes people act weird around you when they think you're famous.

One time I was speaking at a chapel service for a Christian school, and a woman came up to me all flustered and embarrassed. "You are one of my biggest fans!" she gushed.

I snickered, thinking she'd notice her mistake, but she didn't. I think she was hurt when I laughed. "You are!" she said emphatically. "You *are* one of my biggest fans!"

"Oh," I said. "Well, thank you." I was somewhat speechless. I'd never met someone I was such a big fan of before.

Another time a very prim and proper Baptist woman picked me up at the airport to drive me to the event at which I was scheduled to speak. "You're all mine for the weekend," she said as she met me by the baggage claim area.

"I can't wait," I said.

Her hand flew up to her mouth. "Oh, I'm so sorry, I didn't mean it like that!" I thought about sharing this story when I spoke that Sunday morning at her church, but I decided against it.

Once, after speaking at a conference in San Diego, I was walking past some people in the back of the room and heard someone whispering to her friend, "That's Steven James!" I felt ridiculous hearing that. I just pretended I didn't hear them and walked away.

I wonder how anyone could stay human hearing those types of things all the time, being the celebrity, being onstage at the supermarket, at the fitness center, at your kid's soccer game.

"Look! It's Tom Cruise!"

"Aren't you Julia Roberts?"

"Oh, Tiger Woods! Over here! Could you sign this golf shirt for, um . . . for my kid?"

I'm glad I'm not famous like that. I wouldn't know what to do. I'd go crazy or get hooked on drugs or move to Argentina. Or maybe I'd learn to moonwalk and start wearing only one glove around town.

It would terrify me because I know something all those people don't—I know what I'm really like. I know the dark shape of the things that worm their way through my heart. I know the nasty truth about who I am inside—that I'm an impatient, needy, slightly neurotic, moody, manic, cynical, easily addicted, and desperately driven guy.

My wife never whispers to her friends, "Look! That's Steven James!" when I walk past because she's seen me lose my cool with the lawn mower. Instead, when I walk through the door, she hands me a bag of dripping garbage to take to the curb and says, "There you are. Did you pick up the milk on the way home?"

Sometimes I meet famous people and I get nervous myself, so I know how weird it can be. Once I ate supper with a famous author, and he got a piece of salad stuck in his beard. He didn't notice, and no one at our table wanted to point it out to him because he was so famous and we were so in awe. So here's this guy with lettuce hanging from his face and all these people at the table laughing at his jokes and pretending not to see the leaf flapping from his beard all during the meal. Being famous isn't really all it's cracked up to be.

Me, I tend to get spaghetti sauce on my shirt when I eat baked ziti. My kids let me know about it right away. They just laugh and point. "Daddy got a stain on his shirt again!"

So much for feeling like Mr. Famous Author Guy.

Yet here's the thing that's unbelievable to me: God actually knows me, the real me—the slightly neurotic, sometimes cynical, sauce-on-my-shirt me—and he still wants to spend time with me, still wants to hang around with me all weekend. In one of the great ironies of the universe, God—the creator of moons and dreams, the architect of DNA and the Grand Canyon—points excitedly at me from heaven. "That's Steven James!" he whispers to the angels. "That's the guy I was telling you about!"

Me. A tiny speck of a person on a tiny speck of a planet in a vast, trackless galaxy. He knows my name and my heart and my past, and he still loves me. How does that make me feel?

Tiny and huge at the same time.

∽

On top of Haley Pass, a saddle about 11,200 feet up in the Wind River Range next to 12,504-foot Mount Hooker, there's a pile of stones. Apparently, people who make it to the top of the pass add one to the pile.

When I hiked across that mountain pass a few years ago, I thought of adding a stone myself. It was natural, almost instinctive. I grabbed a rock and headed to the pile. There were no signs up there saying, "Put a rock on the pile, dude!" But they didn't need a sign. I just wanted to leave my mark. I guess we all did.

The book of Genesis includes the story of the Tower of Babel, where the people wanted to raise a monument to themselves that reached all the way to heaven. They wanted to make a name for themselves so everyone who followed them would know they had walked on this planet. I guess they heard the same voice in their hearts that we hear today: *Oh, that someone would know I was here! Oh, that I might be remembered!*

Let me make my building two inches taller than yours.

Let me earn one dollar more than the next highest paid wide receiver.

Let's race so we can see who wins.

Let's count up the sales receipts to see who's number one this quarter.

Let me place my stone on the pile; build a pyramid, a skyscraper, an empire; write a novel; sign my painting. It's why we stick a flag on the moon, carve our initials into trees, get personalized license plates, donate money to get our name on a brick, write graffiti on bathroom walls, put name plates on our desks, and leave our life dates etched on our tombstones. A friend of mine told me about a surgeon who got caught engraving her initials in her patients. We want people to know we were here. We want to leave our footprints on this planet or at least our initials on someone's intestines.

I thought about some of those things as I stared at that pile of stones and felt the untamed ancientness of the mountains all around me.

Finally I decided if I put my rock back where I'd found it, I could write about it someday to show how humble I was. So I put it back and started to descend the other side of the mountain. And that day I noticed the trail was very steep and my footing uncertain all the way down.

> the wax is melting again.
> i feel myself plummeting
> toward the sea.
>
> no, i do not blame
> poor icarus for
> his curiosity.
> i too would have flown
> too close to the sun.
> and still do
> > nearly every day.

～

I don't think we understand humility very well. The last thing most guys want to be known for is being meek. I mean, how many college football coaches include that in their pregame speeches? "All right, guys, I want you to go out there and show 'em what a little meekness looks like! I want humility, you understand me? Compassion! Love! Sacrifice! Now go out there and be meek like you mean it!"

Yet Jesus said, "Blessed are the meek, for they will inherit the earth" (Matthew 5:5 NIV). The guys who'll win the final trophy will be the humblest ones on the playing field. The meek will indeed one day conquer the earth.

So what does true humility or true meekness look like?

A couple of times at my creative storytelling workshops I've invited participants to act out Jesus's parable of the proud Pharisee and the humble tax collector (see Luke 18:9–14). First, I have all the women stand and take on the role of the proud Pharisee. "Act proud!" I tell them, and their noses go into the air, their eyebrows rise, and their hands snake to their hips with an attitude. We don't have any trouble identifying what proud people look like.

Then I tell the guys to act like the humble tax collector, and almost in unison they fold their hands behind their backs, lower their eyes, and stare at the ground as they slowly rock back and forth like a bunch of oversized metronomes.

"I said act humble," I say, "not like you just lost the basketball game. Go on, act humble."

And they stand there and stare at me, confused. They have no idea how a truly humble man should stand or act or talk or live.

What does humility look like? Where can I find a model of meekness to emulate? How would a truly humble man stand? I wish I could tell you the answers, but the truth is, I'm as clueless as all the other guys standing there staring down at their shoes trying to figure it all out.

I looked up the words *humility* and *confidence* in a Bible concordance. As I was paging through the verses, I came across these words: "Such confidence as this is ours through Christ before God. Not that we are competent in ourselves to claim anything for ourselves, but our competence comes from God. . . . Therefore, since we have such a hope, we are very bold" (2 Corinthians 3:4–5, 12 NIV). Whatever true humility does look like, it's not afraid to be confident too. Apparently, we're supposed to lead boldly meek lives.

∾

A few years ago I was at Mr. K's used bookstore here in Johnson City, and I found one of the books I'd written on the shelf. At first I thought it was pretty cool to see the spine of my book on the sales rack at a bookstore, but then I realized I was standing in a *used* bookstore.

Unbelievable! Someone had unloaded a book I'd written, a book I'd sweated over and lost sleep over and spent half a year of my life crafting word by laborious word. Some lowlife had sold my masterpiece to the guys at this bookstore for pennies on the dollar.

I picked it up and flipped it open. Whoever had owned the book had taken really good care of it; the pages were barely worn. It didn't look very "used" to me. I don't think it had ever been read.

Then I turned to the dedication page in the front of the book to see if I'd signed it to anyone and discovered that this was the copy I'd given to my daughters' babysitter. Here's what I had written to her:

Dear Eileen, (no, I'm not going to tell you her real name)
Thanks for babysitting and loving my girls!
May 2001
Steven James

I told this story one time at a writer's conference, and the entire audience gasped because they knew authors would rather be boiled alive in yak fat than find someone who didn't appreciate their writing as much as they do.

I stuck my babysitter's autographed book back on the shelf and went to see a movie where I could fume in private and clench my teeth for two hours without anyone noticing. I'm not sure if I was feeling meek about then, but I do know I wanted to kill someone. In a Christian way, of course.

For some reason I'd thought that *my* books didn't deserve to be in a used bookstore, that *my* books should be immune from that fate. That *my* books are literary treasures, keepsakes suitable for framing, and ought to be placed in time capsules so that people twenty thousand years from now can see the pinnacle of twenty-first-century literary prowess. I have this picture in my mind of these little shrines in people's homes where my books are carefully preserved, and as the proud owners walk past, they genuflect and offer up a moment of silence to the author. Ohm. Ohm. Things like that.

Finding that book in the used bookstore was a brutal reminder that everything I do is temporary.

One day all of my books will be out of print, all of my stories will be forgotten, all of my words will turn to mist. When I die, only a few people will notice. I'll get one little paragraph on the obituary page, but even that'll end up at the bottom of someone's birdcage within a week. Solomon noticed how absurd it all is, "Like animals we breathe and die, and we are no better off than they are. It doesn't make sense" (see Ecclesiastes 3:19 CEV). Whether it's tomorrow, or in a dozen years, or in a hundred, there'll come a day when no one remembers my name.

Except for Jesus.

And I wonder, should that make me feel tiny, or huge?

∾

Sometimes I have a hard time figuring out whether or not Jesus was humble. I mean, he actually told people that he was humble and gentle of heart. Usually the minute you claim to be humble, you aren't anymore. I think there's a rule about it somewhere, like an eleventh commandment or something: *Thou shalt seek humility but never claim to have found it. If thou claimest such, then thou art no longer humble but haveth too biggeth a head.*

Yet Jesus told the people: "Let me teach you, because I am humble and gentle, and you will find rest for your souls" (Matthew 11:29).

Once I was reciting some Scripture verses at our church for a Christmas service, and I had to say those five words of Jesus: "I am humble and gentle." When I got to that part, I could almost hear the people who knew me snickering. The phrase "I am humble" just didn't sound authentic coming from my lips. I just couldn't figure out the right inflection. At least I was doing it as part of a drama and not actually saying the words about myself: "Hey, kids, your daddy is a very humble man!" Or to my wife: "Good morning, sweetheart. I'm feeling very humble and gentle today, can you tell?"

I think Jesus was the only person to ever live who actually knew the right way to say those words.

And yet, when Jesus challenged the people to find anything wrong with either his life or his teachings, they couldn't do it (see John 8:46). That doesn't seem like a very humble thing to say: "Go on. Find something wrong with me—if you can. Later I'll be signing autographs; please, no pushing in line." (Okay, I'm paraphrasing, but you get the point.) The best his enemies could do was complain about his use of metaphor when he said he was going to raise the temple (meaning his body, not their worship center) three days after they destroyed it. For this they lobbied to have him put to death. Nice.

Of course some people didn't like that Jesus claimed to be their Savior. The folks in his hometown were offended when he told them he was the living fulfillment of God's centuries-old prophecy. "Who does this guy think he is?" they muttered. "Isn't he the carpenter from down the street?

sailing between the stars

Aren't his brothers and sisters around here somewhere? Where does he get off claiming to be so high and mighty?" (see Mark 6:2–3). But even here it's not Jesus who ends up looking arrogant but the people. It doesn't seem proud for Jesus to make those claims—just honest.

Jesus had a lot to say about humility; it seems his followers needed to hear about it on a regular basis. "The greatest among you must be the servant of all," he told them when they were arguing about which of the twelve apostles was the greatest. "Since I've washed your feet, you ought to wash each other's feet," he said when they forgot what a life of service really looked like. One time he warned them to watch out for those who like attention and honors (see Mark 12:38–40). And once he directly addressed those who like attention and honors: "When someone invites you to a feast, don't take the seat of honor. Instead, take the seat no one wants. For the proud will be humbled, and the humble exalted" (see Luke 14:7–11).

Most churches I visit have reserved parking places for the pastors—of course they're the most coveted spots right up close to the building. I wonder sometimes whose idea it was to reserve those spots, the pastor's or the flock's. I have my suspicions. I don't think I've ever visited a church where the parking spots reserved for the staff were the ones no one else would want, way back at the far end of the parking lot. Church people typically park as close to the building as they can and then sit as far back from the preacher as they can. Lutherans and Baptists might not agree about the finer points of water baptism, but from what I've seen they're on the same page when it comes to the Doctrine of the Close Parking Spot and Back Pew Theology.

Yet Jesus says, "Don't sit in the seat of honor. Don't exalt yourself. Be humble." It seems like such a simple concept—stop exalting yourself and putting yourself above others. And then Paul has to complicate matters even more by writing to the believers in Philippi, "Don't be selfish; don't live to make a good impression on others. Be humble, thinking of others as better than yourself" (Philippians 2:3). So now we're not just supposed to avoid selfishness; we're actually supposed to think of others as better than ourselves.

Verses like those make me think about the clothes I wear, the car I drive, the house I own. After all, most clothes, cars, and homes are designed to draw attention to the owner, to make a good impression. But humble people don't draw attention to themselves; they don't live to make a good impression on others. What does a humble person dress like? What kind of a car does a humble person drive? What would a modest home look like?

This teaching of letting other people have the coveted spot has sweeping implications for merge lanes, last-minute Christmas shopping at Wal-Mart, and last-cookie-on-the-tray etiquette.

It also brings up some obvious and rather troubling applications in various fields of life including sports and competition, business, marketing, public relations, and (of course) writing. What would it really look like to live a life in which you weren't trying to exalt yourself but were working instead for the good of others? Promoting your competitor's product (or book) above your own? Helping them succeed rather than trying to get ahead of them?

What would it really look like to place others first? To serve, honor, and love them above yourself? I'm not sure. But I know it would look a lot different than America looks today.

So one day I decided to start putting Jesus's advice into practice by sitting in the places no one else would want. I parked in the back of the parking lot and it rained. I sat in the front row at church and the pastor made fun of me during the sermon.

This humility thing wasn't playing out quite like I'd had in mind.

That week I was flying to Dallas, so I decided to purposely *not* ask to be seated in the exit row on the flight. If you fly often, you know that the exit row is the only place on the plane—besides first class—where those of us over six feet tall can actually sit without having to chew on our kneecaps. Frequent flyers call it "poor man's first class." Exit row seats are the most coveted ones around.

So on my flight to Dallas I sat two rows back from the exit row. Upon arrival, as I unfolded my body and extricated myself from the seat, I realized my knees hadn't felt that humble in years.

Then before my flight home, I walked up to the Delta ticket counter in the Dallas airport to get my seat assignment. Once again I didn't ask for an exit row.

"Any seat will do," I told the perky-looking ticket agent.

She smiled at me as she tapped away at her keyboard and said, "Well, Mr. James, it looks like you have enough frequent flyer miles, so we're bumping you up to first class."

"What?"

"First class."

I opened my mouth to say, "Um, no thank you. I would like to let someone else sit in first class in the seat of honor today. You see, I'm practicing humility as I seek to more closely follow my Lord and Savior Jesus Christ." But instead I said something else: "All right!"

"You're a lucky man."

"I guess so!"

Since I was sitting in the privileged part of the plane, I got to board before all the little people did. Then a flight attendant with perfect teeth and willowy legs smiled at me and asked if she could get me something to drink. Why, yes. I'll have a cappuccino, thank you.

Soon the people in coach class began boarding. I turned around and watched as they wrestled their bags down the narrow aisle in the center of the plane and then tried to jam them into the overhead luggage compartments that had been specially designed by geeky, sadistic airplane engineers to appear large enough to hold any bag but were actually precisely one centimeter too small for carry-on luggage to fit, no matter how hard you pounded on it. Oh, it was great entertainment.

My bags fit beautifully in the first-class bins, with room to spare.

While I waited for my liquid refreshment, I leaned my seat back and stretched out my legs. I actually had enough room to cross my ankles. In fact, there was so much space between me and the seat in front of me that my grandmother could have parked her Buick in there and not run over my feet.

The flight attendant returned with my coffee and a pair of headphones for the in-flight movie. "They're complimentary in first class," she told me.

"How much would they cost if I was in coach class?" I asked.

"Two dollars."

"All right!" I said. "This rocks!"

Then she took my order for supper. I had to choose between porterhouse steak and grilled chicken drizzled with almond glaze. The people in the back of the plane had to choose between stale pretzels and miniature-sized, chewy granola bars that taste remarkably like wet sand. (This, of course, I knew from many hours of personal experience.)

It was almost enough to make me forget about my resolution to start being more humble. But then about halfway through the flight I had to go to the bathroom, and on my way I noticed all those people who didn't have enough money or frequent flyer miles to get the good seats, all packed into the back of the plane.

I started thinking of what Jesus might have done in my situation. I pictured him going to the back of the plane and finding an elderly man with a walker and a respirator and switching places with him, or maybe finding a frazzled mom wrestling with her toddler and offering to baby-sit for the rest of the flight while she sat up in first class sipping bottomless glasses of white wine. Somehow I couldn't picture Jesus or Mother Teresa or even Gandhi sitting in first class.

But when I was done using the bathroom, I didn't switch seats with anyone. I just returned to my seat and stretched out my legs and ordered another cappuccino.

I discovered that day that I am definitely not Jesus. Or even Mother Teresa.

It's a simple thing, really, to let someone else have the seat of honor. But it's a hard thing too.

∽

Both boldness and humility are hard to figure out. Based on the ads I see on TV, my beer is bold, my coffee is bold, my southwestern cheeseburger has a bold new flavor, my car has bold styling, and I'm dressed in the bold colors of spring. With all that going for me, I must be one bold man.

I know Jesus was bold, but it was in a totally different way.

Jesus told the people that he was humble, but whenever he talked about himself, he used the highest praise possible. John Stott noted this in his book *Basic Christianity*:

> Above all, he was unselfish. Nothing is more striking than this. Although believing himself to be divine, he did not put on airs or stand on his dignity. He was never pompous. There was no touch of self-importance about Jesus. He was humble.
>
> It is this paradox which is so baffling, this combination of the self-centredness of his teaching and the unself-centredness of his behaviour. In thought he put himself first; in deed last. He exhibited both the greatest self-esteem and the greatest self-sacrifice. He knew himself to be the Lord of all, but he became their servant. He said he was going to judge the world, but he washed his apostles' feet.[1]

We think the humble person should stare at the ground and slowly sway back and forth, but Jesus stood tall and took control. He claimed to have the answers, the hope, the relational intimacy with the divine that we all long for. "I am the way and the truth and the life," he told his disciples. "No one comes to the Father except through me" (John 14:6 NIV). "I am the resurrection and the life," he told Martha at the grave of her brother. "He who believes in me will live, even though he dies; and whoever lives and believes in me will never die" (John 11:25–26 NIV). Those are not the words of a guy who just lost the basketball game but of a man who has conquered the world.

Yet his life exhibited a grand humility in which he voluntarily became a servant and then let himself be sentenced to death. Quietly. Humbly. Like a lamb to the slaughter.

This amazing enigma can only be unriddled if he truly was the one he claimed to be. How could anyone other than a God among men live this way and speak this way and transform the lives of billions with his rarified form of bold humility?

Jesus shows us a life of unhalting humility, but in his teachings he is never self-deprecating. He was more like a tempest than a doormat. He always lifted himself up. He is somehow meek and strong at the same time. He let people worship him and affirmed them when they did. He claimed to be equal to almighty God, never admitted to any wrongdoing, declared himself to be God's promised deliverer, claimed to forgive sins, and then performed amazing miracles to back up his claims.

And his followers? Well, after the Spirit touched their lives, they were bold enough to die for their humble Lord and humble enough to give him all the credit for their changed lives.

A few years ago I went on a weekend retreat at a cabin up in the mountains near my home. I was overdosing on the writings of the Christian mystics and got a little caught up in the moment. Before I knew what I was doing, I prayed something like this: *"God, here I am. Do whatever you want in my life to make me more humble. Whatever you need to bring into or take out of my life to draw me closer to you, do it. I'm ready. Do with me*

as you will." I think I'd only had about three hours or so of sleep. That's really the only way to explain a prayer like that.

When I prayed those words, I had no idea God would take answering them so seriously. When I got back home, it took him almost no time to send me friends kind enough to tell me how impatient I can be, how rude I sometimes am, and how I should be a better listener. Then I went to speak at a conference, and when I was done the guy in charge pulled me aside to tell me how disappointed he was in my message and how I'd completely missed the mark and undermined the goals of their entire event for the 1,500 teenagers there. Then I checked my email and found that a book I was certain would sell immediately for an outrageous amount of money had been soundly rejected by nearly every Christian publishing company in the galaxy:

"We didn't feel that the idea was executed as well as it could have been. The ideas seem new and fresh, but the execution fell flat."

"Everything has to really be hitting on all cylinders for it to make it, and I'm not sure this is there."

"At times it gets too 'preachy.'"

"The book just seems to be trying too hard! The author doesn't seem to have a natural connection with his audience, at least in these pages."

Wow. God was really into answering this prayer. Thoroughly.

I'm not sure I'd recommend that prayer to you. God seems all too happy to answer it.

But then again, maybe I would.

Jesus calls us always toward unsettling levels of honesty and humility. "Let me teach you," he says, "because I am humble and gentle." And then he does just that with all who accept his invitation and follow him. He teaches them his unique brand of confident humility—slowly and gently, though, because it takes some of us a while to really learn how to live it out.

I tried showing that kind of bold humility to my office manager. "I'm not trying to brag," I told her, "but I have a hard time finding people as smart as I am."

She just shook her head. "I have to say, sometimes you seem really arrogant."

"Oh."

I guess I've still got a lot to learn about what it means to stand in the gap between boldness and humility, between an awareness of my failures and a confidence in God's grace. I think humility is knowing yourself for who you really are and refusing to hide behind the illusions of who you wish you were. That's a journey that takes most of us at least a lifetime to complete. I've barely made it past the starting point.

Here's what I'm slowly beginning to learn: I can't change myself into someone good enough for God to love. No matter how much self-control I exhibit or what happy feelings I muster up or self-affirmations I utter, I can't become worthy of God's love. I can't become big enough, important enough, smart enough, or good enough to demand his attention. I'll always scribble outside the lines. Always need a little more dung by my roots. No matter how hard I try, I'll never become the kind of person a deity would admire. Maybe that's what meekness is—finally realizing that.

Yet the shocking, unsettling truth is, I don't have to. God has already accepted me as is. He is my biggest fan.

And I don't know if that should make me feel tiny.

Or very, very huge.

beyond the mirage

Back in the 1990s, my friend Jayne went to Guatemala to live for six months with her aunt Jo, who is a nun. When Jayne came back to the states, she told me this story.

"All around you," said Jayne, "you can see green mountains on the horizon. It's hot. You can feel the sun on the back of your neck, and the flies—there are always flies—crawling on your arms. Sometimes you can smell the smoke from the burning rainforests being turned into farmland. And if it's morning, you can hear the singing of roosters and the laughter of children."

One of the girls in the village is named Reinita. Her name means "little queen." She turned seven just before Jayne met her. She lived with her family on the edge of town in a fifteen-by-fifteen-foot house. Her father's name is Pablito. There are seven children in the house, but every day it's Reinita who runs out to meet Pablito when he comes home from the fields.

Most of the people in Yelpimich live in shacks for homes. Most of them are hungry too, and diseases run rampant—diseases like malaria and cholera. Jayne tried to help me understand how dangerous cholera is. "Cholera? Well, you vomit continuously for three days. You dehydrate. And then you die. Almost everyone there knows someone who has died of cholera."

When Jayne visited the town, there was no electricity in Yelpimich and no running water. Even the drinking water was full of parasites. Reinita's family had access to the water trough once every three days. Washing, cleaning, and collecting water must all be done then. "Before that trough was built by the U.S. government a few years ago," Jayne told me, "the villagers needed to walk seven miles for water."

And then she pauses in her story and shakes her head. "But despite the poverty and disease, the people are so friendly. And thankful! So thankful for every day they're alive! They live every day as fresh as if it were their first—and carefree like it was their last. Most of each day is spent on survival; there's no time to wonder about tomorrow, to worry about it or plan for it. No one ever mentions tomorrow."

Most of the people who live in this mountain village where no one ever mentions tomorrow are born here, live here, and die here. Reinita was one of the few who got to leave.

She has a rare blood disease. Jayne might have told me the name for it, but if she did I've forgotten it. I remember that it causes sores on your face and hands. There's a small clinic in Yelpimich, but the nearest doctor is an hour's drive by truck, and the nearest hospital is seven hours away. "Only the rich merchants and the church own trucks," said Jayne. "The clinic and the doctor couldn't help, so two years ago, Jo drove Reinita south to the hospital at Coban."

As they bounced down the road on that seven-hour trip, the little queen asked the nun, "Will I die from these sores on my body?"

Jo was silent for a moment. "Everyone dies, Reinita. Death is a door to heaven. Heaven is on the other side." To a five-year-old, that was answer enough.

The treatments didn't help. Her sores and swelling appeared and then disappeared and then reappeared again and again—each time getting worse. The doctors didn't know what to do.

Then one day when Pablito returned home from the fields, Reinita didn't run out to meet him because she was too weak to stand up. She lay in bed surrounded by her six brothers and sisters when Pablito walked into the room. He knelt down and took her hand.

"Why aren't the roosters singing, Father?" she asked.

"It's not yet morning, Reinita," he replied. "The roosters will sing in the morning."

All that night, Pablito stayed up with Reinita, his little queen. Together they sang songs to Jesus by candlelight.

Later Reinita whispered again, "Why don't the roosters sing, Father?" Her words were much softer now.

"Reinita, it is not yet morning."

Slowly, night gave way to dawn. And as the sun rose, the roosters sang. Pablito carried his little queen out into the morning light, and there in his arms Reinita died—smiling at the rising sun, listening to the song of the roosters.

Jayne finished her story by telling me about a letter Jo had sent to her. "Life goes on in Yelpimich," she said. "Pablito's wife is ill today, so his twelve-year-old daughter is taking care of the five youngest children. While dressing the two-year-old, she noticed the same type of sores as Reinita had before she died. And the roosters continue to sing in the morning."

Reinita was seven years old when she died in January of 1995.

&

When my grandmother died she left me a box of old letters. At the bottom of the box, I found a small photograph of a young Hispanic man. He was maybe seventeen or eighteen years old, dark haired, oily eyed, and very lonely looking. Piercing eyes, sad and deep, stared at me from the faded photograph. No note came with the picture, no name to tell me who he was. The upper left-hand corner of the picture was torn.

At first I was just going to throw it away, but then I studied it again. He looked so lost in the world. I flipped it over once more, thinking maybe his name and identity would have magically appeared on the back in the last few minutes. Nope. Nothing.

I asked around. None of my other relatives knew who he was or why my grandmother had kept the picture.

Why is he so sad? I wondered. *What's he thinking? Who is he? Why did Grandma keep this picture and then pass it on to me?*

I kept that photograph of the boy I didn't know. I don't know exactly why; maybe just to remind myself that he was someone's son. Someone's friend. Maybe someone's lover. And somewhere along the line his story had intersected with my grandmother's story, and then it had entered mine.

Most of the things that are really important to me are only important because of the stories that surround them—the ceramic pitcher my great-great-aunt used to daintily pour me icy water on sweaty summer days, the rubber snake that served as the waterfront mascot when I was a counselor at a YMCA camp back in college, the photograph of my wife and me on a nameless peak in Alaska on our honeymoon. These things only become valuable because I know the stories behind them. Without the stories they're trinkets, knickknacks, flea market fodder. Junk. But because of the stories and memories, they've become treasures I would brave a fire to save.

That torn photo was the only connection I had to the story of that boy until I lost it. Now my only connection is the story I tell to you.

Imagine being in a place where you could look over your whole life at once, seeing it in its entirety from beginning to end, like sitting in a helicopter watching a parade. All the different stages of your life pass by at once: sleeping peacefully as a baby . . . stumbling around as a toddler . . .

losing your first tooth . . . learning to ride a bike . . . sleeping over at your friend's house . . . hoping the kids in junior high won't make fun of you . . . flirting with your high school sweetheart . . . graduating . . . landing that first big job . . . changing diapers . . . dropping your kid off on that first day of school . . . noticing the first gray hair . . . retiring . . . watching others around you die . . . closing your eyes one final time . . .

See the sweep of your life? See how quickly it floats by? How soon the endless night will come?

Now, ask the helicopter pilot to take you up higher. As you rise above the city, you see all the other parades marching toward their conclusions—the parades of your friends, your family, sports heroes, politicians, world leaders, celebrities. More and more lives.

Hundreds.

Thousands.

Billions of lives. All fading away, all coming to an abrupt end. Some after many miles. Others after only a few steps, while everyone else marches on.

When I think of that, it's hard for me to see how anything I do has any lasting importance at all. It's hard to see how anything I do ultimately matters. I feel terribly insignificant in the vast sweep of things, in the sway of the stars and the bosom of space. David felt it too when he thought of the vast galaxies swirling around his tiny soul. "I look up at your macro-skies," he prayed, "dark and enormous, your handmade sky-jewelry, moon and stars mounted in their settings. Then I look at my micro-self and wonder, why do you bother with us? Why take a second look our way?" (Psalm 8:3–4 Message). And it isn't just the brevity of my parade that haunts me, but the looming question of whether or not my life has any ultimate meaning or significance at all.

In the book of Ecclesiastes, David's son Solomon explored this question in depth. But instead of the awe David felt, Solomon saw only futility. The Amplified Bible translates Ecclesiastes 1:2 like this: "Vapor of vapors and futility of futilities, says the Preacher. Vapor of vapors and futility of futilities! All is vanity (emptiness, falsity, and vainglory)."

All is emptiness. Everything is vapor.

> my soul is famished,
>   yet feeds on phantoms.
> i lift another forkful
> of vapors to my mouth
> as my stomach grumbles
> at me, starving for
> something real. the
> more i eat, the emptier
> i become, when my diet
> is made up of so much
> illusion and mirage.

Does progress matter? Not really. Generation after generation comes and goes, and what really changes? Do people benefit from their work? Not really, since we all die anyway. The earth keeps circling the sun, the days swirl by, the wind wanders the world, the rivers flow into the sea, and water evaporates and turns into clouds again—all one big, wearisome cycle. Progress? I guess there's progress in medicine and technology and things like that, but in the end we all die anyway. So what does it really matter?

There's only the endless cycle of life and death. We hunger, we struggle, we endure, we die. "Everything is so weary and tiresome!" wrote Solomon. "No matter how much we see, we are never satisfied. No matter how much we hear, we are not content" (Ecclesiastes 1:8).

What about wisdom or pleasure or hard work or recognition—do any of them matter? Not according to Solomon. He found them all meaningless.

Vapor of vapors. Mists above the sand.

The same patterns keep returning over and over again. The same questions. The same longings. The same discontent. And when you get right down to it, you find people felt and thought and suffered in the very same way long ago, yet because of the meaningless cycle of life, we don't remember them. Their pictures have no labels. Their stories are forgotten.

No matter how hard we try, we'll never right all the wrongs in the world. No matter how hard we look, we'll never find all the answers on this earth. We'll be left with questions and injustice, and if we chase after the answers, we'll come up with nothing but a handful of mist and a heart full of vapor. You can't catch the wind. Chasing it is an endless exercise in futility.

That's what life is. An endless exercise in futility.

We die, the roosters sing, and our families move on.

> and here is the truth from which all others grow. here is the
> spring from which all others flow: soon i will be dead.
> *soon, as measured by stardust and time. soon as measured by comets*
> *and dreams.*
> soon. soon.
> soon, i will be dead.
> and here is the question that decides everything—
> what will i do until then?

ᘐ

While some cultures deal with death better than others, I'd say that overall, as a species, we pretty much stink when it comes to handling death in healthy ways.

I think it's because the human heart was never designed to experience this kind of grief. In the beginning, God created us to celebrate life together with him, not to mourn the loss of each other. Death and decay weren't in the original game plan. They only came later on when

Adam and Eve thought God was holding out on them and decided to take things into their own hands rather than leaving things in his. And we all know where that led.

Our souls weren't fashioned to handle the razor-sharp shards of a broken heart. Nothing hurts more than having to clean up a mess like that. It can be a bloody business indeed. Some of us never recover.

And if it's true that humans are made in the image of God (and I believe it is), then God was never intended to grieve either. Hearts like his, like ours, were never meant to be pierced with the pain of saying a final good-bye.

So here's what we do: we play pretend. We refuse to talk about death, and we act like it'll never happen to us or the ones we love. We rarely plan for it, prepare for it, or expect it.

And we invent safe little euphemisms—he passed on . . . she didn't make it . . . the cancer was fatal . . . I'm afraid the illness is irreversible—and create clever ways of keeping up the facade that we're never going to die. But it's all an artful fraud.

I was on an airplane and the flight attendant started going through the pre-flight spiel, instructing us on what to do "in case of a water landing." I looked around. We were on a 747 jet. This plane is not equipped with pontoons. A 747 does not "land" on the water. It explodes on impact into pieces the size of my toenail. The proper way to prepare for an event like this is not to stick your head between your knees (as if there were room to do that anyway) but to scream until your throat bleeds and pray in six languages at once.

I arrived home (without experiencing a water landing, thankfully) and turned on the TV, and a commercial came on for life insurance. This guy walks onto the set all somber-looking and explains the benefits of their policy. Then he says I should sign up so my family will be taken care of "in case the unthinkable should happen." Of course, by "the unthinkable," he means "in case you die."

But the thing is, death isn't unthinkable; it's inevitable.

What kind of culture calls things that are inevitable *unthinkable*? What kind of world refuses to think about what is certain but instead spends its time worrying about things that are not?

But I guess even though it's inevitable, death *is* unthinkable.

That's the thing. That much is true.

Sometimes I cry when I watch movies. Not often or anything. It's not like a big problem, and I usually hide it when I do, but sometimes I cry. Yet the weird thing is, I almost never cry in real life. When I jam my finger playing basketball, I act tough. When one of my books gets a miserable review, I go and build something with a hammer and lots and lots of helpless nails. But I don't weep. Even when I find out someone I know has died, I don't usually cry. I get really quiet. I feel bad about it. I don't know what to say. But I don't typically cry. At least not right away.

On December 26, 2004, an earthquake that measured 9.0 on the Richter scale rocked southeast Asia near the island of Sumatra, sending out a series of tsunami waves traveling at 500 miles per hour. At first the reports said 12,000 people were killed. Then 24,000. A few days later they thought it was 45,000. Then 76,000. Then 155,000. Every day the total rose. On January 25, 2005, it was up to 288,000 people. Later I heard it might be half a million. And in the weeks that followed the tragedy, I found myself turning on the news to see what the new number was. But I didn't cry.

I was talking with my friend Jason about it, and I shook my head and mentioned I hadn't cried yet. "What's wrong with me?" I said.

He was quiet for a moment, and then he said, "Whatever's wrong with you is wrong with me too."

In her stunning book *For the Time Being*, Annie Dillard writes, "What were you doing on April 30, 1991, when a series of waves drowned 138,000 people? Where were you when you first heard the astonishing, heart-breaking news? Who told you? What, seriatim, were your sensations? Who did you tell? Did your anguish last days or weeks?"[1]

I'll bet most people anguished just long enough to flip the channel to the next episode of *Seinfeld*. Or maybe they popped in a movie and broke out the tissues.

Whatever's wrong with them is wrong with me too.

❧

I can't figure out why people cry at the movies but not at real life. Why do we cry over something we know isn't true and fail to cry over a tragedy that is? As I write this, every day 153,417 people die on this planet. That's 107 people per minute. How often should I mourn? How long should I grieve for each one of them? How many of them deserve my attention when they pass into infinity? No one ever teaches you that sort of thing in school.

My friend Mike died in 2003, the same week the space shuttle *Columbia* exploded trying to reenter the atmosphere over Texas. No one reported Mike's death on the news. No one wrote columns about him. No committees were set up to investigate the cause of his death. Instead, our nation spent the next couple weeks mourning the death of its heroes. But how long should I mourn for those seven astronauts compared to the other 153,410 people who die each day? How many tears should I shed for each of them?

I don't remember where I was when I heard about the space shuttle tragedy, but I can't seem to forget standing there in the parking lot staring at the ground as my wife softly told me that my friend Mike was dead.

Instead of learning to deal with death, we teach our children how to diagram sentences, tell the greater-than sign from the less-than sign, and download ring tones for their cell phones. Important stuff like that.

she sits near me and twirls her gray hair.
and she laughs to herself.
no one else in the coffee shop is laughing.
one man is jabbering into his cell phone, another guy
is studying a medical textbook,
several people are staring off into space, sipping coffee.
a couple of others talk with each other in hushed tones. and nod.

we're all lost to each other as she sits among us mumbling
enjoying her own private joy.
and i wonder what in the world she's laughing at.

but now, a moment later, she's crying.

and i already know people don't cry in public. not like this.
something must be wrong with her.
she must be one of Them.
yes, something must be wrong with her. after all.

or maybe, just maybe, something is right with her,
and something is wrong with the rest of us.
who sit here and neither weep, nor laugh,
at this awkward world we call home.

Someone told me that God mourns over everyone who dies, and I believe her. After all, if God cares enough to know how many hairs are on my head, he must certainly care enough to cry when my heart plays its final note. That means that 107 times a minute, God feels the searing pain of losing a child.

When they showed Jesus where his friend Lazarus was buried, Jesus wept, and the people said, "See how much he loved him" (John 11:36).

Me, I cry in the movies but not in real life.

I heard somewhere that the human heart contracts one hundred thousand times a day.

It's curious to me that we talk about our hearts contracting and expanding. I certainly know what it feels like for my heart to contract. I just wish it would expand, truly expand, more often.

∾

I went to hear a renowned author speak at our local university a few years ago. After the lecture, he opened up the floor for questions from the audience. Someone stood up and asked him, somewhat tongue in cheek, "What's the answer to the meaning of life?" He paused for a moment and then said, "Our lives are only a momentary splinter of light between two eternal darknesses. I have no answers."

As I recall, that put a bit of a damper on the Q&A time.

I wonder how I would ever motivate myself to write if that were my view of life. I wonder how I would be able to keep the bottle of pills far enough from my reach day after day.

In his search for meaning amidst the seeming futility of life, Solomon found every avenue of life full of vapor except for one. And that road gave meaning to all the others. "Everything you were taught can be put into a few words: Respect and obey God! This is what life is all about" (Ecclesiastes 12:13 CEV). And, of course, John reminds us that to obey God is to love him (see 1 John 2:5). So finding and living out the love of God brings substance to even the most vaporous aspects of life.

Without God at the center of the universe, without his smile on the edge of dawn, life would all be vapor and mirage. But when he's present, all of life becomes drenched with possibility; every moment becomes lined with purpose.

light splinters shadows
stars pierce the night.
dawn sweeps the skyline
blisteringly bright.
a smile from a stranger
a hand upon mine
a child at the breast
of a mother in line.
marvel in moments
of the most common kind.
a world of wonder
that awakens my mind.
hope for tomorrow
in the hope of today.
we glisten, we flicker
we explode from the clay.

The thief comes to steal meaning and moments away, but the Son comes to fill empty lives with the wine of God's presence. "My purpose is to give life in all its fullness," said Jesus in John 10:10. Jesus gives meaning to the mundane, a purpose to my dreams, a depth to my knowing, a reason for my suffering. Jesus is the missing ingredient that makes all other aspects of life make sense.

My daughters once got onto a science fiction movie kick. They watched the first five Star Wars movies in a two-week span. Eden, who was five at the time, went up to Liesl and said, "We have to get a dog, Mommy!"

"And why is that?"

Eden got a distant look in her eyes and said, "It's my destiny!"

At that point we realized she'd been watching way too much Star Wars.

One of the most incredible characteristics of God is his timelessness, his eternal, unchanging nature. To us time unfolds moment by moment. To us the future hasn't happened yet, but God exists in every time that has ever been, is, or will ever be. What we call *foreknowledge* is simply God's awareness of what's existing to him right now, in the time known to us as the future.

This realization helps me to better grasp the concepts of destiny, predestination, and God's sovereignty. Since he dwells in the future as much as in the present, every choice we will ever make is already known to him. And because of that, he also knows the results of those choices. He sees the entire parade at once. When Eden asked for a dog, God already knew we would end up with a shy sheltie named Sassafras who likes to eat shoelaces and thinks the cat is an overgrown chew toy.

I believe God knows all that there is to know in the universe. He knows who will seek him and who won't, but this knowledge doesn't limit our ability to choose how to spend the moments he gives us. Whether we get a dog or not is still up to us. Despite what my daughter might think, it's not up to destiny.

And here's the other thing: to God there is no then. To him it is always now. And because of that, this moment offers all that he has to give, all the love that the universe has to offer.

The idea that every moment, every life, every encounter could ultimately matter is the most ludicrous and necessary idea in the world. As soon as one life becomes expendable, all lives become expendable. As soon as one moment doesn't matter for eternity, the meaning of every moment is brought into question. But if this moment is from God and for him, nothing is a means to an end. And if everyone's destiny matters to Jesus, no one is a means to an end.

When I finally see that, a timelessness sweeps over me, borne of beauty and perspective. I realize, *I am small. I am part of this world. I am a thread in a magnificent tapestry.*

there is a moment beyond this moment.
i finger it, fragile and delicate and hopeful,
torn sweetly from the fabric of
the robe of time. i touch it, glancing
my fingertips across its promises.
and something stirs deep within me
    wondering,
        buoyant,
           and wild.
    could it be that
    everything really matters?
the wind tastes like
spring-flavored freedom
this time of year.

Life isn't simply a futile journey toward becoming fertilizer; it's the chance to dance toward eternity, hand in hand with the Poet of Time, while his stars, the glimmering jewelry of the night, wink at us from the sky.

One of my favorite promises from the Old Testament comes from Malachi 4:2: "But for you who revere my name, the sun of righteousness will rise with healing in its wings. And you will go out and leap like calves released from the stall" (NIV).

I can't think of a better definition of life than that: to leap wildly in the love of God. This is the God with unfailing love who keeps track of all our sorrows and collects every one of our tears in a heavenly bottle (see Psalm 56:8). This is the God who puts so many of my scribbled pictures on his fridge: "The LORD your God is with you, he is mighty to save. He will take great delight in you, he will quiet you with his love, he will rejoice over you with singing" (Zephaniah 3:17 NIV). I can hardly fathom that God even notices me in the vast sweep of time and space, let alone that he takes great delight in me and rejoices over me, dancing through the courtyards of heaven singing my name. My soul is dizzy with the thought of it. My heart begins to believe in tomorrow again.

I'll admit that the idea that God has a place in his story for each one of us is a bit absurd. But if God is real, what's the alternative? In other words, what kind of God would he be, if his story *didn't* include each of us?

To some people the idea that God would love us each enough to shape his story around us is folly. To others it's evidence of a troubling, resonant love. As Annie Dillard wrote, "Only some deeply grounded and fully paradoxical view of God can make sense of the notion that God knows and loves each of 5.9 billion of us."[2]

I can't make sense of it, but I can believe it. And I can bet my life and my eternity on it.

Here is the ultimate paradox of divine love: we *do* matter to him. His heart is bigger than the Milky Way, and yet every breath we take matters to our Maker. Every life on this planet matters, from me to Pablito to a nameless boy in a faded photograph to a little queen dying in a shack in the jungle. We're sailing not from darkness to darkness but toward the Starmaker's open arms. Tiny and huge at the same time.

Here is the meaning of life: a candle flickers in the night. The roosters rise to sing. A Father carries his child outside to welcome the coming dawn.

The door swings open again.

the glass isn't half anything

I had a rather troubling dream one night. When the alarm clock buzzed, I hit snooze, rolled over, and told my wife I'd just dreamt about her. She sighed, snuggled close, and smiled. "Oh, that's so nice."

"Do you want to hear about it?"

"Of course."

"Well, in my dream, these aliens attacked our city with a giant tank thing and shot this laser beam out, and you fell down, and I told the kids, 'Run over there! Quick! Be safe!' And I leaned over and noticed that the blast from the aliens' tank had turned some of the bones in your face to mush."

She blinked. "My face was mush?"

"Well, yeah. Now, most of the people thought the aliens were friendly, but I didn't. I mean, when someone shoots a bone-melting ray at your wife's face, you don't put 'em on your Christmas card list! That's what I say!"

She stared at me quietly in the early morning light. "Then what?"

"Anyway, I scooped you up—without any regard for my own personal safety, I might add—and I went sprinting through the city looking for a doctor."

"Well, that's a little better."

"And then, there's a short transition in my dream, I can't really remember exactly what happened next, but then I was playing golf." I paused.

"Okay," she said slowly. I noticed she wasn't snuggling quite so close anymore. "And what ever happened to me?"

"I don't know. That's when I woke up."

"My face was melting off and you went to *play golf*?!"

"Um, I looked for a doctor first."

She made a sound in the back of her throat that didn't sound like laughter. "The next time you dream about me, I don't wanna hear about it unless it has a happy ending." Then she rolled over to go back to sleep.

I decided not to tell her how I did in the golf game.

Inexplicable means "unable to be explained or accounted for." It's a good word to describe human beings being human—our dreams, both while we sleep and while we're awake, are inexplicable and agathokakological. Of course, *weird* would be another word for us, but it's not nearly as impressive to use in Scrabble. (Okay, I admit the transition right there was a little weak, but I've been wanting to tell this alien ray face-melting story for years, and I couldn't find any other place to fit it in. Most editors would have ruthlessly sliced it from the text, but mine is just too, too nice. So don't email her about how lame this transition is, it's all my fault.)

My uncle worked as a school counselor. One day the custodian at the school he was working at was quite upset. He led my uncle to the boys' bathroom and pointed at the wall. "What do you think we should do about that?" he asked.

"About what?"

"Can't you see? One of the students urinated on the electrical outlet!"

"And?"

"And the last school counselor who worked here told me if a kid ever did that, he was suicidal!"

"Huh," said my uncle. "I guess that's possible, but it seems like an odd way to try to kill yourself. Maybe he was just curious, or someone dared him to do it, or maybe he just has bad aim. People do stupid things sometimes. There's not always a good reason for why we do stuff."

And this from a psychologist.

Sometimes we're just curious. Other times we're confused, or trying to prove ourselves, or whatever. And sometimes we just have bad aim. Sometimes dreams and life make sense; most of the time they're as inexplicable as we are.

∾

When you think about it, it's kind of funny, us trying to explain God. As little as we understand ourselves, how could we ever hope to comprehend a God who tosses galaxies aside with a flick of his finger and genetically engineers a billion species of interdependent life in a couple of days in his spare time? How can the pottery know the mind of the potter? How can the pine needles know the pattern of the roots deep beneath the soil?

Mystery is so wedded to Christianity that we hardly even notice the obvious miracles.

For example, when Moses asked if he could glimpse God's face, the Lord told him that no one could do that and live (see Exodus 33:20), yet think of all the people who gazed into the face of Jesus and then went home to tuck their kids into bed at night. We remember the miracle of the fish and the loaves—the day Jesus fed five thousand hungry families with two fish sandwiches—but we forget the greater miracle that no one died that day as they watched him bless the food.

And every time someone comes to faith, God is raising another dead spirit to life. Dead bodies coming to life make front-page news in our world, but tell someone that you were once a dead spirit who has now been awakened by almighty God, and my bet is you'll find yourself standing alone at the office Christmas party.

One of the deep enigmas of God is this: he is always available, yet not very visible. He hasn't filled the world with overwhelming proof of his existence, just hints of his presence. Paul wrote, "Since the creation of the world God's invisible qualities—his eternal power and divine nature—have been clearly seen, being understood from what has been made, so that men are without excuse" (Romans 1:20 NIV), but how can that be? How can God's *invisible* qualities be *clearly seen*? I love how David explains it in Psalm 19:1–4:

> The heavens tell of the glory of God.
>> The skies display his marvelous craftsmanship.
> Day after day they continue to speak;
>> night after night they make him known.
> They speak without a sound or a word;
>> their voice is silent in the skies;
> yet their message has gone out to all the earth,
>> and their words to all the world.

They tell the story, but we don't listen. How long has it been since you listened to the poetry of the skies or heard the stars whisper tales of Christ in the night?

Miracles leap at us from every nook and cranny on the planet. As Walt Whitman wrote, "A mouse is miracle enough to stagger sextillions of infidels."[1] This universe is full of whispers of God's mystery, his presence, his character. But most of the time we're too blind to notice.

out here, the sky spans my wonder.
out here, the stars cut the night.
i can feel the heartbeat of thunder
    and the pulse of all that is bright.
out here, the wind has no master.
out here, the day wears no chains.
i inhale both glory and disaster,
    peace is part of the moment that reigns.
mountains rise to scratch at the heavens,
eagles circle and plummet and soar.
valleys dip with rivers like ribbons,
    and i learn what i've known before.
i'm touched by the hand that's above me,
i'm moved by the Spirit within.
in this moment i know that he loves me.
    the Artist has painted again.

The wild thing is, so much of what is real lies beyond the realm of our senses. In fact, all the things that matter most—love, justice, peace, truth, and so on—are known only by the ripples they create in the world; they can't be either proven or discovered solely through the senses. Just like the wind rippling across the water, you can see where they've been, but they remain invisible. God ripples through our lives every moment, but frozen souls have a hard time noticing.

"God's ways are as hard to discern as the pathways of the wind," wrote Solomon, "and as mysterious as a tiny baby being formed in a mother's womb" (Ecclesiastes 11:5).

So in the end, explanations always fall short, and we're left with a choice between sight and faith, between practicality and belief. Because beyond the world that we see with our eyes is another world that pulses beneath the skin of the visible— a world of prayer and spirit, of love and the future, of wonder and ultimate reality. And that world is even more real than ours since it's only because of the invisible that the visible is even here.

∾

Christianity is a religion of extremes, of powerful and opposing truths that smash together in spiritual fusion. It's very unsettling. Christianity is an invitation to everyone to drink more deeply of life, but that includes both the most delicious and the most bitter flavors it has to offer.

In *Orthodoxy*, G. K. Chesterton explored the idea that Christianity is both more optimistic about life than the optimists claim and more pessimistic about life than the pessimists believe. And yet the two ideas don't cancel each other out like we'd expect, but rather they reveal each other in sharper contrast than in any other religion—because Christianity actually tells the truth about the world.

Okay, I admit it: I had to read his chapter a couple of times before I caught on to what he was talking about. But the more I thought about it, the more I agreed. The cynic always finds something to complain about, the optimist something to be thankful for. The first is distracted by the depths of darkness; the second is misled by the splendor of the light.

The Christian looks at this inexplicable world and sees both the darkness and the light, often in his own heart at the same time. He both cringes and rejoices, he both weeps and laughs, because at last he's beginning to see himself and this ludicrous, agathokakological world as it really is. And how else can you respond to a world that's full of both death marches and wedding dances, arsonists and saints, bubble gum and tear gas, stretch marks and dimples, birth announcements and obituaries?

We are the supernatural, soul-birthed children of God living in a world of hair balls and pink slips.

life is splendor and magic,
toenails and dandruff,
wonder and love and mistakes.
it is both glorious and tragic
to live on this planet of
teardrops and angel food cakes.

This is the world of brittle dreams and broken hearts and rainbows in July. A place of acute pain and resonant joy. Just ask anyone who's been on a honeymoon or lost a child—they'll tell you about the extremes.

The more I've thought about Chesterton's observation, the more I've come to believe that there are really only three ways to respond to our world. The first way, of course, is denial. Some of us deny the daily ache of life on this planet; others among us ignore the glory. That's why some people still don't believe the Holocaust happened. It's just too terrible to be true—but it is true. And denial is also why some people can't accept God's unconditional love. It's too good to be true—but it is true. They're both true.

I'll bet you know some people who only see the pain and not the beauty. Over time they've become skeptical, cynical, and hollow. You can see the hopelessness in their eyes and hear it leak out around the edges of their words as they share dessert with you at the coffee shop down the block.

Other people ignore the pain and pretend there's always a bright side of life. They're the ones who think if we're just nice enough to the terrorists, they'll be nice to us in return. Maybe we can all join hands and dance around the campfire with Cindy Sheehan singing "Give Peace a Chance." But the problem is, right in the middle of the hug-fest, someone's going to sneak up from behind with a stiletto and slit your throat. Because that's the kind of world we live in too. Full of both good and evil. Unable to be explained or accounted for.

Jesus told his friends to be as innocent as doves and as shrewd as snakes. After all, it's a snake-eat-dove world out here, and each one of us has both the scales of the snake and the wings of the dove in our souls. We are serpentine. We are avian. We are both the dancers by the fire and the assassins with knives drawn, lurking in the shadows.

Of course, denial means closing one eye to reality. It means ignoring either the miracle of the mouse or the pain of the miscarriage. I suppose we all do our fair share of this as a way to cope because sometimes denial seems like the only way to make sense of life. How could life have so much hope *and* pain? I think one of the reasons Jesus came was to open both of our eyes to the stunning, breathtaking, heartrending realities of life and eternity.

sometimes i want
to go deeper into
the silences of God;
but sometimes the
silences are so deep,
they threaten
to swallow me up.

the truths of the Son
finger their way through
my heart, leaving
bloodstains and blossoms
wherever they pass.

If denial doesn't work, we might try to turn down the volume of both the pain and the glory. Go for a middle-of-the-road approach. By muting both the sharpest screams and the wildest laughter, we can pretend things aren't nearly as bad as they seem or as good. This is the approach most Eastern religions take.[2] In order to make sense of the suffering in the world, Buddha taught that we should look at it as an illusion. But the problem is, pretending that suffering is an illusion doesn't cure Alzheimer's or make the tumor go away. Any way you cut it, both shipwrecks and sunsets cover our planet.

It just doesn't make sense that life could be both this magnificent and this terrible, yet it is. People really do live in palaces. People really do live in garbage dumps. Those of us who live in middle-class America tend to believe the illusion that this is a middle-class world, but it is not. It is a world of great poverty and great wealth, great pain and great peace. Ecstasy and oblivion.

The only option left is to accept the paradox that our planet is somehow full of tearstains and giggles, delight and despair. It's an all-of-the-above world.

The poet Robert Bly beautifully noted the paradox of this world's sadness and splendor when he wrote of "the puzzled grief we all feel at being appointed to do mysterious tasks here, on this planet, among mountain meadows and falling stars."[3]

In the end, the glass isn't half empty or half full. It's not half anything. Life is both more full than you'd ever expect and more empty than you can imagine. Lift the strange cup of reality to your lips, look closely at the world for yourself, and you'll see what I mean.

And once again, Christianity offers the reason why: God offered wonder, we chose pain, and now our world is woven with both. This planet is immersed in the paradox of good and evil and has footpaths that lead to both paradise and the inferno.

And try as I like, I can't make sense of it. But you know what? God doesn't ask me to. He isn't offering me a horoscope or a fortune cookie so I can decipher life. Instead he's offering himself, to lead me by the hand through all of the messiest and richest depths of mystery, misery, pain, and glory this planet has to offer.

Christianity is both meek and wild, full of doctrines that can be neither tamed nor denied. It's not nice and its teachings are not safe, as Chesterton discovered on his journey toward faith: "It was no flock of sheep the Christian shepherd was leading, but a herd of bulls and tigers, of terrible ideals and devouring doctrines, each one of them strong enough to turn to a false religion and lay waste the world. . . . This is the thrilling romance of Orthodoxy."[4]

The Christian runs through life's center with both eyes wide open. Here is our chance to admit all of the greatest and most troubling truths about life. Christianity looks like a strange beast only because it is a true animal, and truth is always stranger than any fictions we could ever hope to make up.

Each moment is a window from heaven that opens to both exquisite pain and incredible pleasure.

> so how could these both grow ripe and strong:
>   a funeral dirge and a wedding song?
> to everyone brave enough to eat
> this life is both succulent and
>   bittersweet.

∽

I really shouldn't admit this, but when it comes to cars, most guys are completely clueless. We don't have any earthly idea what the stuff under the hood really does. It's all very fascinating to us, of course. Sometimes some of the stuff gets hot and greasy, so that's pretty cool. And things move around in there too. I think they're called pistons, although I don't really understand what they have to do with basketball.

The more gifted among us actually know how to check the oil level. The rest of us are pretty much in awe of them. But of course, we would never dream of admitting any of this—especially to another guy. Instead, we flip open the hood and tap things with a screwdriver and point at stuff that has wires attached to it. "Mmm . . . yeah, looks like yer defibrillator belt is a little worn down there by the, uh, exuberator combustion modulation chamber."

And the other guy nods knowingly. "Yep. Yep. I was just thinking the same thing myself, Lenny. The exact same thing."

This pretending is less painful than actually admitting how clueless we are. About cars. About life.

Unable to be explained or accounted for.

Just like my dreams, my uncle's students, my world.

But that's okay.

Maybe someday I'll be able to look back and see the route up the mountain, and it'll all make sense to my head rather than simply to my heart. Until then I'm caught up in the thrilling romance of dancing with a rugged bridegroom toward the edge of eternity amidst the weird dreams, bad aim, and indecipherable miracles of life.

thirteen

chewing on God

Hunger spoke to me.

"Come and dance with my possibilities! Leap into the depths of my sea! Grab handfuls of my soil and cover yourself with my children!"

I shrank back. "No! How could I? You call me to indulgence, but the saints preach abstinence. You call me to gluttony, but the monks teach moderation!"

And she replied, "Don't be afraid of me! I'm as natural to you as your birth. Who doesn't desire breath? Who doesn't desire life? Who doesn't hunger for food for the body and bread for the soul? You're a child of your hungers. Hunger wakes you up and moves you through your day. I'm not your enemy but your friend. I'm your guide to all of life."

But I shook my head. "Then why do the prophets and the mystics warn me of you? Why do we pray for self-control? Why do we fast except to show that we're not enslaved by our hungers but free to serve God? Why do some teach that the removal of all desire is the greatest pinnacle of truth?"

"The removal of all desire is emptiness and nothingness," she said. "That's not truth. That's not enlightenment; that's darkness. Truth always fills and reveals; it never empties and removes. I don't call you to gluttony but to life. I don't call you to indulgence but to fulfillment. Who gave you your hunger? Who lined your throat with thirst? Who wedded desire to your soul?"

So I asked, "Do you speak of the Master, the Almighty, the Creator of All There Is?"

Hunger nodded. "Never call unclean what God has called clean. Never call impure what God has called good. Your hunger he created. Your hunger he blessed. Your hunger he himself embraced when he stepped onto the earth as a man-child."

I still didn't really understand, though. I'd always thought that hunger was like a wild dog that trotted by your side and needed to be tamed and leashed, not allowed to run free. "But isn't spirit better than matter?" I asked her. "And aren't the disciplines of the heart purer than the hungers of the flesh?" I had to ask the question, though I knew many had asked it before. Perhaps, finally, Hunger could teach me the answer.

"Ah," said Hunger, "then why didn't the Master create only spirit? Why did he create matter at all? Not only that, but more matter than spirit? And why did he call all he had made—not just the spiritual—good? Your hunger for food is good. Your hunger for beauty is good. Your hunger for life is good. Your hunger for sex is good. Your hunger for meaning, peace, love, joy, and God are all good. Physical desires aren't aberrations of your spiritual self but extensions and expressions of your true self."

And I wondered if Hunger could in fact be speaking the truth. If so, it was a deep truth lost somewhere in the dust of the ages.

"Never think of yourself as more than human," she continued, "or less than spiritual. Both are lies. Remember that without hunger you wouldn't survive. Hunger is a clue to your needs. Your spirit isn't more real than your body; your body isn't more real than your spirit. But *you*! You are more real than both, for both are within you and about you. You are flesh and blood and the breath of God. You are the soil of the divine will. What do you hunger for in life?

"You desire food—enjoy it!

"You desire peace—pursue it!

"You desire drink—consume it!

"You desire wonder—embrace it!

"Need is the bed of desire. Don't shut her in the room alone and starve her or you'll starve yourself. Go to her. Sleep with her. Hold her and love her. She is your partner—I am your partner—in life. I am wedded to your soul."

So I listened to Hunger, and I let her inform me. And sometimes she fulfilled me, and sometimes she misled me. And sometimes I mistook her for Greed or Envy or Lust.

But still, I became more human each day. My soul grew as round as the sun and my spirit began to climb toward the edge of the sky because I listened to Hunger that day.

And now she trots by my side without a leash. And I follow her nose through the forests of life.

It's hard to know what to do with our God-woven hungers. The truth is, it's very easy to let them become distorted or skewed or out of perspective. It's easy to get confused because in the interplay of body and soul, we are more than just meat and more than simply spirit. We have both physical needs and divine leanings with desires that stretch in every direction. We are earth and we are sky; starlight and soil searching for both enlightenment and a warm slice of deep-dish pizza.

what i do not see
is as real as what i do
see. the invisible world
embraces the visible.
the supernatural is bride
    to the tangible.
touch.
caress.
tremble.
    in the mingling
of their hearts and the
union of their vows,
the two have become one
    in the soul of the seeker.
and they refuse to divorce
each other, despite how
awkward and fumbling
their union
can be.

We want to relax, make love, eat hot dogs, lose weight, or move to Albuquerque. We long to be accepted, fulfilled, loved, enlightened. We long for peace, transcendence, a touch of the divine. As the Pulitzer Prize–winning poet Charles Wright wrote, "We yearn to be pierced by that occasional void through which the supernatural flows."[1]

And it isn't just that we want some of these things; we shape our entire lives, dream our whole futures around obtaining them. Our souls wither without them. And all of those desires of the body and longings of the soul, woven together, make us human.

Of course, some people look down on the physical desires, while others ignore the spiritual. Ascetics deny themselves pleasure; hedonists deny themselves self-control. So each become less, not more, than their truest selves. Because both pleasure and self-control are vital ingredients in being human.

> "i'm heading out in search of my fortune," i said, "just like in the fairy tales."
>
> and i met the elf who offered me magic beans, and the witch who offered me an apple, and the wolf who gave me directions through the forest.
>
> and i saw the castle rise through the thicket and i touched the tip of the unicorn's horn and i heard the howl of the werewolf and somewhere along the way i found my fortune and chopped down the beanstalk and became a man and married the princess and moved into a palace.
>
> but i'm still waiting for the happily ever after part to come true.

Deep questions accompany deep hungers. So most of us come to the point sometime in our lives when we ask, "Is this really all there is?" And behind that question lurks a deep, haunting disappointment with the world.

This is fascinating to me. Why would that be? No matter how much fame, talent, wealth, or influence we attain, we just can't find enough to make us ultimately satisfied. A profound longing for something more gnaws at us all. Yet no one is reassured by the belief that this world is all that there is. I've never met anyone who puts the question like this: "Aren't you glad this is all there is?" People who believe there's nothing more than this life don't find satisfaction, but only despair or resignation. Why would humans have such a universal disappointment in the world unless they were made for something more than this world?[2]

Just the fact that we seek enlightenment, by whatever term you want to use, is an admission that we're currently in the dark. No one seeks endarkenment, after all. Our world already has plenty of that.

I believe that our longings for mystery, wonder, adventure, belonging, and love are part of the fabric of being human—a vital part. After all, God has "planted eternity in the human heart" (Ecclesiastes 3:11). And if we have eternity growing in our hearts, how could we ever expect to find fulfillment by clutching only the things of this world that are so . . . temporary?

Yet in a sense we're temporary too. We're both momentary and eternal. It's all very confusing to me on a day-to-day basis. Sometimes I end up trying to feed one hunger with the wrong kind of food. And sometimes I still confuse my deep hunger for the holy with my appetites for pleasure, intimacy, sex, fulfillment, and Cool Ranch Doritos.

And here's another problem. In John 4:14 Jesus said that when we taste of him, we will never thirst again. But the thing is, when I taste of the divine, I *do* thirst again—I'm hungrier than ever for him. He satisfies me but leaves me more dissatisfied than ever. He both quenches my thirst for the celestial and whets my appetite for heaven. Somehow he both douses the fires inside of me and kindles them to a roaring blaze. Ever since I first tasted the glory he offers, I've never been so easily satisfied again.

And I've found that if I don't feed on him, take my sustenance from him, devour him deeply into my heart, my soul will continue to hunger for the mystery of God's presence (see Matthew 4:4).

Starving souls don't need food or porn or Marlboros or Miller Lite. We need to feed on the very words, the living story, of God. "Taste and see that the LORD is good," wrote David in Psalm 34:8. And when I taste even a small portion of the mystery, power, and peace that come from nourishing my heart on God, I always want more.

For me it's like eating chicken fajitas at my favorite Mexican restaurant. I enjoy every bite and always want one more forkful. Getting even just one bite of Jesus makes me want to engorge myself on God's love.

When Jesus broke his body and poured out a sparkling cup of his blood for his followers to taste at the Last Supper, he was offering them a chance to take part in the deepest mystery of all—a mystery that nourishes the soul's primal hunger.

Even today believers can encounter the mystery of Christ's presence with our tongues, our throats. We can feed on the holy and find a way to satisfy our innermost cravings.

I have to admit, though, it doesn't always seem all that holy or satisfying. Sometimes the bread is stale, and most churches these days substitute grape juice for wine. Having juice and crackers feels more like snack time at preschool than a foretaste of heaven.

And some churches don't treat the meal very sacredly at all. "Oh, yeah, it's been a couple months. We oughtta do that again." Others turn it into just another ritual.

All of this, of course, ruins the taste of it for some people. Sometimes for good.

I've been there too, making light of the power of this meal. But these days, whenever I'm tempted to give up on the essence of this mystery, I remind myself that God is a meal I was never meant to taste with my tongue alone but also with the rich taste buds of faith.

In one of the oddest things Jesus ever said, he invited people to feed on him, the living bread from heaven: "Those who eat my flesh and drink my blood have eternal life, and I will raise them at the last day. For my flesh is the true food, and my blood is the true drink" (John 6:54–55).

"Devour me," he says, "and you will live forever."

I won't even try to explain all that this talk about chewing on God might mean. I'm no theologian. I'm probably more confused about it all than you are.

But from my own life I do know that sampling his presence awakens deeper hungers and stronger thirsts than I ever had before, yet also brings a strange quietness and contentment. In those times when I actually do place my lips against the words of Jesus and devour them deeply into my heart, I find both a peace that cannot be described and a longing that cannot be filled with anything but him. As St. Augustine put it so elegantly in his *Confessions*, "You called, you cried out, you shattered my deafness: you flashed, you shone, you scattered my blindness: you breathed perfume, and I drew in my breath and I pant for you: I tasted, and I am hungry and thirsty: you touched me, and I burned for your peace."[3]

We eat his body and remember his Spirit.

We drink his blood and taste his forgiveness.

This is part of the glorious mystery of panting for God. Psalm 42:1–2 says, "As the deer pants for streams of water, so I long for you, O God. I thirst for God, the living God." To encounter Jesus is to finally taste of eternity (see John 17:3). And when your soul licks that, everything changes—both the things that you ultimately hunger for and the appetites your soul begins to have.

He fills our hungry souls and at the same time awakens new hungers that lead us deeper into the spiritual life and the untamed realms of being fully human, for our hungers are both gifts and hints.

The God who invented taste buds and hunger pangs offers us plates at the feast held in his honor, waiting just beyond the curtain of eternity. And he's inviting us to join him at the banquet table.

this is a strange kind
of love—the beach
    offering itself to the pebble.
the tree giving its life
    for the leaf.
what kind of galaxy is this
where love is so
backward and inverted
    and fulfills my hungers
    by awakening such
    deep and echoing desires?

fourteen

dance of the wills

Zach had a pretty good life. Sure, he cooked the books a little, did some creative accounting now and then, didn't report *all* of his earnings, but that stuff was only to be expected of someone who worked for the Jerusalem branch of the Roman IRS. *"Hey, what do you want from me? I'm just trying to make a living here. And besides, I'm not as bad as most people!"*

But still, most of the other Jews—especially the churchy, religious types—wanted nothing to do with him. They knew he padded the books and ripped them off to line his own pockets.

Then one day Zach heard about a local preacher who seemed to really enjoy hanging out with tax collectors. Unlike most religious people, this guy wasn't ashamed to be seen with them, to joke around with them, or even to enjoy a night out on the town with them. Hmm. Curious. Unlike the other religious teachers in the community, this guy seemed to actually *like* tax collectors. Interesting. A little weird.

So Zach decided he wanted to see this Jesus character for himself. You may have heard the song about him in Sunday school:

Zacchaeus was a wee little man and a wee little man was he.

He climbed up in a sycamore tree, for the Lord he wanted to see,

But as the Savior passed that way, he looked up in the tree

And he said, "Zacchaeus, you come down!

    For I'm goin' to your house today;

    I'm goin' to your house today."

(The song has hand gestures and everything, but they're kind of hard to translate into print. They're worth learning, though. Kind of like the "YMCA" song for three-year-olds.)

The point is, when Zach went looking for Jesus, Jesus was the one who found Zach. And before Zach could even say a word, Jesus invited himself over for supper—which, incidentally, was a big deal in those days. Back then, eating supper with someone was a way of accepting them. You didn't share meals with people you didn't want to become friends with.

And then, right there in front of everybody, Zach entered the kingdom of heaven. "Zacchaeus stood there and said to the Lord, 'I will give half my wealth to the poor, Lord, and if I have overcharged people on their taxes, I will give them back four times as much!'" (Luke 19:8). That was also a big deal. A very big one. He opened up his heart and his life and his home in one grand gesture. He let God in, committing himself to a new life of repentance and restitution.

His new life showed that he was a true child of God. And when Jesus saw Zach's change of heart, he said, "Salvation has come to this home today, for this man has shown himself to be a son of Abraham. And I, the Son of Man, have come to seek and save those like him who are lost" (Luke 19:9–10).

In this wonderful little narrative, both Jesus and Zach made choices that drew them closer to each other. Jesus came to seek the lost; Zach went in search of Jesus. There at the sycamore tree, Jesus found Zach and Zach found Jesus. And when Zach responded by following Jesus's teachings,

Jesus celebrated his decision. It was a dance of the wills. Step and stride, slide and twirl. Jesus and Zach two-stepping toward eternity.

Everywhere you look in Scripture, you see this drama of conversion occurring. The dance of the divine in someone's life—God seeking and choosing, people accepting or declining, because when God comes a-courtin', some people walk off the dance floor and head off alone into the night.

But sometimes people do take his hand and step with him into the heart of the music. And that's when the real dance begins.

For years I've been interested in this riddle of us seeking the God who's also seeking us. Who ultimately does the finding? I think the question is fascinating. And apparently I'm not the only one.

It is so important for every soul among you who is seeking God to realize that He was first in the field, and was seeking you, or ever you began to search for Him. . . . There is no worse crime than to take to oneself the credit for even a little of the grace one has received. You could not have sought the Word . . . if He had not sought you.

Bernard of Clairvaux (1091–1133), saint[1]

For Thou didst first stir me up that I should seek Thee.

Thomas à Kempis (1380–1471), monk[2]

"All who seek me find me," your Word says. But are we not seekers because we have already been found first by you? And do we not find you because it is you who have first loved us?

Then seek us, O Lord, until we are completely found. And draw us close with your love until we find you forever.

Michael Card (1957–), songwriter[3]

This attracting spirit is no other than God himself, who, in drawing us, causes us to run unto Him.

Madame Guyon (1648–1717), mystic[4]

The Inviter does not wait for those who labor and are burdened to come to him. He himself lovingly calls. He himself comes. He follows the urging ache of his heart, and his heart follows his words, "Come here!"

If you follow these words, they in turn follow you back again into his heart.

Søren Kierkegaard (1813–1855), philosopher[5]

As for this "finding" of God, we cannot even look for Him unless we have already found Him, and we cannot find him unless He has found us. We cannot begin to seek Him without a special gift of His grace; yet if we wait for grace to move us before beginning to seek Him, we will probably never begin.

Thomas Merton (1915–1968), comtemplative[6]

Before a man can seek God, God must first have sought him . . . God takes from us every vestige of credit for the act of coming. The impulse to pursue God originates with God, but the outworking of that impulse is our following hard after Him; and all the time we are pursuing Him we are already in His hand. . . . To have found God and still to pursue Him is the soul's paradox of love.

A. W. Tozer (1897–1963), pastor[7]

The more I love You, the more You pursue me with Your relentless love.

Francis de Fenelon (1651–1715), priest[8]

It is the drama of the lost sheep wandering in the wilderness, restless and lonely, feebly searching, while over the hills comes the wiser Shepherd. For His is a shepherd's heart, and He is restless until He holds His sheep in His arms. It is the drama of the Eternal Father drawing the prodigal home unto Himself, where there is bread enough and to spare. It is the drama of the Double Search, as Rufus Jones calls it. And always its chief actor is—the Eternal God of Love.

Thomas R. Kelly (1893–1941), missionary[9]

You didn't choose me. I chose you.

Jesus of Nazareth in John 15:16 (0–33–forever), Savior

From every corner of Christianity comes the same refrain—from Protestants and Catholics, mystics and theologians, philosophers and poets: to find is to be found, to seek is to be sought. For our souls are not the only ones who are restless. God is restless too, even more than we are, for the day when we finally find ourselves in him.

The mystery at the heart of conversion begins with the fact that our souls aren't in touch with God as they should be; our lives are not in tune with his tale. Between us and God yawns a deep valley caused by our greed and addictions, envy and pride, lust and selfishness, rudeness and prejudice and spiritual stupidity. Yet some people do find the king-dom of God and the freedom he offers. So how is the canyon between his holiness and our failures crossed? Who bridges the gap? If we share his story with a crowd of thousands, perhaps a handful will accept it. So why those and not the rest?

so i get this invitation in the mail, right?
and it says there's this party and everything,
and it's supposed to be totally awesome
but i'm just not sure i can go, you know?
'cause i'd have to, like, skip *american idol*
or tape it or something, and then totally
clear my calendar for like the next billion
years or so. and i'm just not sure i'm
ready for that kind of commitment.

Christians have wrestled for centuries over the thorny issue of free will—how God's sovereignty and human responsibility relate to each other. It boils down to this: if God is all-powerful and wants all people to be rescued, why aren't they? Are our wills more powerful than his, or do we lack any free will at all?

All brands of Christianity acknowledge that people are saved by the grace of God—they just don't always see eye-to-eye on how much of a role (if any) we play in the dance.

Some believers say we're free to accept or reject Christ's offer of salvation. Others believe that we don't have any free will at all but that, bound in sin from birth, we are saved (or condemned) solely by God's preordained choice.

Still others say that if we're saved, God gets the credit, and if we're lost, then we're the ones to blame. St. Ambrose, one of the early church fathers, held to this view: "He [Jesus] would never come and knock at the door unless he wished to enter; if he does not always enter, it is we who are to blame."[10]

Each camp has a whole arsenal of Scripture verses that they pull out to debate, debunk, and discredit the competition. Sometimes the attacks can get pretty personal. I've read the stuff, and frankly, most of it I wouldn't recommend. All too often, along with their detailed dogmas come clever ways of interpreting the verses that don't seem to support their views. Sometimes there's so much spin going on to make a Bible verse fit their theology that it reminds me of a political debate gone bad.

Personally, I'm glad it's so puzzling. I'm intrigued by the mystery of it all. The questions, not the explanations, are what draw me deeper into the wonder of the dance.

i seek soul water
where shall i go?
where shall i drink?
where does it flow?

i seek soul water
to quiet my thirst
that rises within me
both final and first.

i seek soul water
to bubble and rise
through heart
and through fire
to finger the skies
　　to quiet my thirst
　　oh, where shall i go
to find soul water
in these moments i know?

Jesus promised that all who seek will eventually find (see Luke 11:9). In his words he echoes the sentiment of Deuteronomy 4:29, in which Moses reassured the Israelites that "if you search for him [the Lord] with all your heart and soul, you will find him," and Jeremiah 29:13, where God told his people, "You will seek me and find me when you seek me with all your heart" (NIV).

And yet Paul points out that no one seeks God (see Romans 3:11) and emphasizes over and over that we're not saved by the things we do and can't earn heaven on our own; in fact, we're dead and doomed forever because of our many sins (see Ephesians 2:1–5). And how can the dead seek anything?

Jesus observed that "the gateway to life is small, and the road is narrow, and only a few ever find it" (Matthew 7:14). He didn't say, "Only a few are found by it." So the search goes on.

James 4:8 tells us, "Draw close to God, and God will draw close to you," yet Jesus pointed out that no one comes to God unless the Father himself draws him (see John 6:65), while the writer of the book of Hebrews tells us to "draw near to God with a sincere heart in full assurance of faith" (Hebrews 10:22 NIV).

Step and twirl. Join the dance.

Jesus preached repentance; he called people to follow him, deny themselves, take up a cross, forsake the world, and believe in him. He never said, "I'd ask you to believe in me, but actually you can't really do that because you're too sinful and it's all up to God to work faith in your heart anyway. So forget it." All of Jesus's calls to discipleship and faith are volitionally based. And when it comes to our wrongs, God never says, "Since you don't have any free will, I'll overlook that little indiscretion." Instead, the choice of accepting whether or not to take his hand and step into the dance seems to be left up to us.

Jesus invites but doesn't bully or manipulate hesitant souls: "Look! Here I stand at the door and knock. If you hear me calling and open the door, I will come in, and we will share a meal as friends" (Revelation 3:20). Sure, he knocks, but he doesn't kick down the door.

God's Spirit is always available for those interested enough to ask for it, but the asking is part of the dance: "If you sinful people know how to give good gifts to your children, how much more will your heavenly Father give the Holy Spirit to those who ask him?" (Luke 11:13).

It seems that it's only possible to enter God's story when he draws me into it, but it's also not possible to enter without the submission of my will to his.

∾

I should mention that it seems pretty clear to me that God's Spirit is the one who gets the credit for rescuing me. After all, a guy saved by CPR doesn't brag about how he "accepted new life" but gives all the credit for his new life to the paramedic who saved him. So that's me. Jesus did CPR on my soul.

I'm also aware that when we try to explain too much of the mysterious interplay of God's will and our own, we run the risk of saying too much or too little. Whenever you talk of mystery, heresy is only a heartbeat away. I've seen some people end up blaming God for not doing enough to save the lost and others end up giving too much of the credit to themselves for entering the dance.

So what exactly is our role in accepting the gift God offers? Is faith the hand that accepts the gifts of God? And if so, do we hold it out to him, or have we stuffed our hands so deeply into our pockets that he has to yank our hands out first before he can hand new life to us?

There seems to be both a divine wooing and a human willing in this process. Yet God is always the one leading the dance.

> love trembles
> before me,
> just out of reach
> and i wonder
> if i'm really
> reaching out for
> it, or if love is
> somehow
> reaching out
> for me.
>
> connection.

∞

It's fascinating to me that when Jesus spoke to Zacchaeus, he said that he'd "come to seek and save those like him who are lost" (Luke 19:10).

He didn't say "*were* lost." Zacchaeus was still as lost as ever, but now he was *also* found.

Recently I read Brennan Manning's book *The Ragamuffin Gospel*, and I highlighted this line: "At Sunday worship, as in every dimension of our existence, many of us *pretend to believe* we are sinners. Consequently, all we can do is pretend to believe we have been forgiven."[11]

The first time I read those words, I thought of someone I knew who really needed to hear them. But, of course, whenever you see someone else's face in a quote like that, it's always a sign of your own blindness rather than their lostness.

As I reflected on Brennan Manning's observation, I got to thinking about Jesus's story of "the prodigal son." It's probably Jesus's most famous parable and very likely his most universally misunderstood one.

Here's the context (you can find the story in Luke 15). Jesus was partying with sinners (again), and the religious people were shaking their heads at him (again). "What kind of a guy is this who eats with people like that?" they were saying.

So Jesus told them a threefold story of a shepherd looking for a lost sheep, a woman looking for a lost coin, and a father who stays at home while his son leaves to squander the family fortune on wine and women. Jesus ties the three threads of his story together with this refrain: "In the same way, there is joy in the presence of God's angels when even one sinner repents" (Luke 15:10).

It's significant that the shepherd and the woman search, yet the father of the lost boy doesn't. You'd expect him to leave home and look for his son, but he doesn't. He just stays at home with the boy's older brother. So there seems to be a huge disconnect between this last story and the first two since the shepherd, the woman, and the dad all represent God.

Then after the wayward son loses his fortune, he decides to return home. Most people think this is the repenting part, but the guy doesn't return home because he feels sorry for anything. I know Scripture says

sailing between the stars

he "came to his senses" (Luke 15:17). But it's his stomach, not his heart, that was sorry. He said to himself, "At home even the hired men have food enough to spare, and here I am, dying of hunger! I will go home to my father and say, 'Father, I have sinned against both heaven and you, and I am no longer worthy of being called your son. Please take me on as a hired man'" (Luke 15:17–19). He decides to return home and confess his sin just to get a meal, not to ask for forgiveness. This guy's not repentant; he's just famished.

So then, as he approaches home, his father runs out to meet him. (Okay, I'll grant that this could count as a search by the father, but stick with me. I don't think this is the search Jesus is emphasizing.) His dad welcomes him without any recriminations and throws a party. At last, the older brother comes home from work, and when he hears who the party is for, he refuses to go into the house.

Now here's where I think the real story unfolds, because at last the dad does go searching for a lost sheep. He goes outside to invite the older brother in to the party. He goes looking for a lost son after all; it's just not the son we thought was lost. We thought this story was just about the first son, but really it's even more about the second.

This isn't a story about Them. It's about us. The one partying with prostitutes isn't the lost son Jesus is talking about in his story. It's easy to miss this. I missed it for years myself. Jesus's real story is about the one who refuses to be found. The one like me, who sees other people as the ones who need Jesus. The one who refuses to enter the party with all those "sinners." The one who argues with his dad until at last the shepherd leaves his sheep on the porch because it isn't willing to climb onto his shoulders and go home.

Then Jesus stops the story before any real resolution occurs. We never find out what the older son does—if he enters the party or not. The father has done his part. He has searched, found, invited. But the lost son's choice is what determines the ending of the story.

Will he enter the dance or not?[12]

As long as we're able to point a finger and shake our heads and see people as *them*, we won't be able to enter the party ourselves.

After all, there is no them. I am one of them. You are too. We all are. Zacchaeus was lost. I am lost. We're all lost. Each of us is the kind of person our mothers warned us about. And it's the most freeing and troubling thing in the world to realize that. Because when we do, we can finally find our place in the story and have a chance to decide whether or not to enter the party for ourselves—whether or not to take the outstretched hand of the Father and let him lead us into the living room where all the other sinners are already slam dancing with their Savior.

Here's where all this hits home: I'm lost but also found. Yes, part of me certainly wants what God wants, but the part that wants what I want is there too and wants to take over and squish the other part, the God part, like a cockroach on the bathroom floor.

The lost think they're found; the found realize how lost they are.

I think as we search for the truth we discover that it's really God who has been pursuing us all along. Here is the narrative of conversion boiled down to its bare essentials:

We run; he seeks.

We seek; he finds.

We find; he welcomes us into the party.

When I was in fifth grade I would always go over to my friend Eddie's house for sleepovers. Then, when it was time to go back home, my mom would come over to pick me up, but Eddie and I would run off and hide somewhere while our moms sat in the kitchen talking and calling for us every few minutes. But we wouldn't come. This was our way of getting to play longer.

By hiding like this, we could draw out the picking-up-Steve time by up to thirty minutes. Oh, we thought we were so clever. We thought we had them so fooled.

Then one day we hid in the closet, and we had to talk in whispers, and my mom didn't come looking for us but sat sipping cup after cup of coffee with Eddie's mom. Time dragged on and on. It wasn't so much fun sitting in the closet after a while. We got cramped and bored.

After nearly an hour, we finally came out of hiding and joined our moms in the kitchen. After all, it's only fun to hide as long as you know someone is looking for you.

Nobody wants to be left alone in the dark.

Of course, maybe my mom knew that if she kept calling for me I wouldn't come, but if she was just patient and waited long enough, I'd finally come to my senses.

∽

The more I think about faith, the fewer things I can think of that I believe in, that I've actually chosen to believe in.

I don't hear Christians talk about this aspect of faith much. I wrote in *Story: Recapture the Mystery* that there comes a day for each of us when faith becomes a choice, but I'm not sure I phrased that right. I think clinging to our beliefs is a choice, but more often than not, it seems that my beliefs choose me, not the other way around.

Some of the things I know, I don't believe, and some of the things I believe, I don't know. For example, I know I'll die someday (perhaps today), but I don't really believe it. If I did, I'd live today differently than I do.

On the other hand, I believe the sun will rise tomorrow morning even though I can't be sure of it. And this is one of those things I don't choose to believe; I just do. I don't choose to believe in things like gravity or justice or New Zealand, but I believe they're real, even though I've never seen them for myself, only evidences of them.

Sometimes evidence and argumentation and logic help shape my beliefs, and sometimes they don't. For example, I believe (and I know I'm in the minority here) that the earth was created in six literal days (gasp!) as Genesis chapter 1 explains. I don't believe in billions of years of macroevolution. I just don't buy it, even though I find some of the evidence offered for the theory to be rather compelling.

And lots of times I believe things I can't prove—like that Jesus is alive today, that no one else is controlling my thoughts, and that all animals go to heaven. I can't prove any of this stuff, but I believe it.

And through this maze of faith and belief, I find that *trying* to convince myself of something only makes it harder to believe in it. Real faith usually comes only when I stop trying. Beliefs choose me.

I think salvation comes when God tells my heart to believe and then shows it how.

∽

Last Halloween I heard a radio commercial for a "Judgment House" that a local church was putting on. Basically the idea is to scare the hell out of people. Literally. It's like a haunted house that tells the story of what will happen to you if you don't "trust in Jesus Christ as your personal Lord and Savior." (According to the sponsors of this event, you have to pretty much use those exact words. And you have to really mean them too.)

So the commercial comes on: scary music. Chains. Screams. The sound of a car accident. (Note: almost all of these "what will happen to me after I die?" skits start with a car accident—apparently that's the only way Christians die—so if you're ever at a church and they do a car wreck skit on stage, be forewarned, you know where the service is going.) Enter a voice: "I know you prayed that prayer," he says, "but did you *really mean it*?" Wicked laughter. More chains. More screams.

I sat there in my car asking myself how a person could know if he really meant it. In other words, how sincere do you have to be about entering the dance? One hundred percent? Is that even possible? I don't think I've been one hundred percent committed to anything or one hundred percent certain of anything in my life. I don't think anyone other than Jesus has ever been one hundred percent sincere.

So then, maybe 99 percent sincere? Is that enough? Will that get me to heaven? What about those who are 82.7 percent sincere? What if I *want* to really believe but can't seem to? What if I'm only 3.1 percent sincere but I want to be around 92 percent or so? And if it's up to me to really mean it, where does grace fit in? I thought we weren't saved by our own effort—how does this sincerity thing mesh with that?

This much I do know: if my rescue depended on my sincerity, I'd be dead in the water. I could never be sure I'd been sincere enough because I know my heart and how mixed-up my motives and goals can be. But if my rescue rests on God's unfailing love instead, I can actually be confident and assured that I'm already at the party. Already home.

As hard as I try or don't try, as sincere as I am or I'm not, I just can't conjure up faith by my own will and desire. I either believe something or I don't. And when it comes to entering the story of Jesus through the mystery of saving faith—this dance with the divine will—that kind of faith *has* to be a gift in some sense, especially to someone as stubborn and oafish as me, or I'd never accept it. It's born not out of my sincerity but despite my insincerity. It comes poking through the crust of my hardened heart because the Spirit gives life and without him I can do nothing, believe nothing, seek nothing at all.

Whenever I'm tempted to try and understand God, I remember Jesus's words, "Just as you can hear the wind but can't tell where it comes from or where it is going, so you can't explain how people are born of the Spirit" (John 3:8). So the dance of life is as mysterious as the wind twirling through the trees, and we're never going to be able to grasp all of its nuances.

I read somewhere that *spirit* means *breath*. The wind of the Spirit is God's breath in my soul.

I love the simple wisdom of Dag Hammarskjöld's observation:

When he saw them all flee,
The skunk decided
He was the King of Beasts.[13]

We see God dance in our souls and decide we're the sincere ones—bunch of skunks that we are. We can't help but get a skewed view of reality since we see everything through our own self-absorbed eyes and motives.

Picture a magnet and a piece of metal on the table. The closer the magnet gets to the metal, the more it draws the metal toward itself. Now, if that chunk of metal could think for itself, it might reason, *Huh, the closer I get to that thing, the more I want to be near it. And since it looks like a chunk of metal, I must be a magnet! Cool!* At first this reasoning seems logical, but the conclusion is actually the opposite of the truth. The metal has everything reversed.

When it comes to spiritual matters, I'm like that confused chunk of metal.

After all, it's the one being drawn. It has no power on its own. Even the longing it feels to be close to the magnet comes from another place—the magnet. I believe that even the desires we have for God are gifts from him to us. I long for him, but all the while it's God drawing me. God is the magnet, and the longing I feel for him is really an extension of his longing for me, rising up in my soul. I feel myself being drawn across the table toward eternity, but even this longing comes from another place.

I was thinking of this mysterious interplay of grace and free will, of the dance of new life and how pilgrim souls finally find their true home, when I wrote this fable:

The craftsman fingered the flute he had just made. "My child, you're newly born, but already pregnant. You're pregnant with wedding songs and funeral dirges and the lyrical tunes of the traveling bards. The music of the world lies in your heart, and the songs of the ages sleep in your soul."

And the flute was silent in reply to all his words.

"Ah, how could I expect you to answer me?" he laughed. "You're empty and haven't yet learned to sing. But now, the waiting is over." He lifted the flute to his lips and added, "It's time to give birth to a song!"

And he began to play.

And as his breath gave life to the song, the flute finally replied to her maker. And her song was sweet and the melody was alive and she brought tears to the eyes of the old man, even though he was the one who played the music and he already knew the song.

Still, she made him cry.

Just as he had designed her to do.

The party has started. I can hear the music floating out the window. The invitation has been offered, and I'm standing on the porch, staring at the open door. I see his hand outstretched toward me. Will I join the dance?

In moments like these, I feel the craftsman lifting me to his lips again. I want to play the music he designed me for, but I can only do so when his breath finally fills my soul.

Only then, when his lips kiss new music into me, am I truly and most deeply found.

— fifteen

the monk, the chainsaw, and the king tut life-sized sarcophagus cabinet

There's a joke about three guys stranded on a desert island. They find a bottle with a genie who offers them each one wish. The first guy wishes that he's off the island and back at home with his family. Zing. He's gone.

The second guy wishes he's back at his job at the sub sandwich place in the mall. Zing, he disappears. Well, the third guy thinks and thinks about his wish until finally he just sighs and says, "I don't know what I want . . . I just wish those other guys were here to help me decide."

Zing.

A friend of mine told me that the Inuit Eskimos have a curse: "May you get everything you wish for."

It's a curse.

∿

Last year my pastor gave a series of messages on being a good steward. He emphasized that we don't own anything, not really, but that in the end we're all just managing God's stuff. As a result of his talks, a group of teenagers and college students at our church started raising money for a mission trip by selling T-shirts that said: "ION—I own nothing."

"You have to get one!" Bug called to me as I walked past the sales table. I've never heard anyone call her by any other name. Bug has more energy than Jackie Chan after drinking a few too many espressos.

"I'll have to think about it, Bug," I say, because saying "I'd feel like a hypocrite wearing that shirt without living it out" sounds like a little too honest of a thing to say in church.

Bug nods enthusiastically. "Okay! I'll be waiting!" Her hair flies everywhere. It's as much in love with life as she is. Sometimes I wonder what it would be like to watch Bug brush her teeth.

One time on a backpacking trip I met a monk. We were both taking a break along a trail in the Shawnee National Forest in southern Illinois. His name was Mark.

Monk Mark.

He was maybe twenty-five or so and looked like he might have been a graduate student studying English comp if he hadn't become a monk. Mark told me he didn't own anything. He'd taken a vow of poverty.

"Then whose is that?" I asked, pointing to his backpack.

"It's the monastery's. They own it. I'm just using it."

Apparently the monks could request things from the guy in charge of the monastery's money, and if it would benefit the community, then he might buy it. There weren't any guarantees.

"Does anyone else use it?" I asked.

"There are a couple of us. We take turns."

They take turns. How nice. "So you don't own *anything*?" It was a setup question, of course.

"Nope."

"Then what about your deodorant or toothbrush or underwear? You don't share that stuff, do you?" Ha. I had him now. I could feel it.

Mark just looked at me like I was a complete idiot. "No, we don't share that stuff. But we don't own those things either. The monastery does. All we do is use them."

Oh.

Mark told me that the monks pool all their resources and do what benefits their community rather than just themselves. And then, when they're done with something (like when they die or grow out of their clothes), they just give that stuff to someone else. All this taking of turns and sharing of things and thinking of others began to sound to me an awful lot like what we teach our kids in kindergarten but then don't actually live out ourselves when we get old enough to buy and keep stuff (like cars and homes and backpacks) of our own.

"Share your toys," we tell our kids. "Be nice."

"Keep out!" we put on our signs. "Personal property!"

I thought of Mark recently when I needed to cut down a tree in the woods behind my house. I don't own a chainsaw, so right away I thought I oughtta go buy one. But then I remembered Mark's backpack (I mean, the one he was using). Take turns. Share. Hmm. Why not.

So I called my friend Dan and asked if I could borrow his chainsaw. "Sure, no problem!"

The next Sunday Dan brought his chainsaw to church and handed it to me in front of the information booth in the lobby right before the service. One of my pastors stood there staring at us the whole time. "I don't even want to know," he said. "Please don't tell me. I don't even want to know." I've developed somewhat of a reputation at our church. I think it started with the sermon on joy.

So I brought Dan's chainsaw home and started working at the tree, but the blade wasn't sharp enough. I couldn't even cut halfway through the trunk. I got more and more frustrated until I found myself saying words to that chainsaw that are not found in the Bible.

If I had my own chainsaw I could take care of this so much easier! I thought. *Mine would be sharper! Mine would be better!* I don't know why I thought that if I owned a chainsaw it would be sharper than Dan's was. Probably for the same reason I buy DVDs when I could rent them. *If I own it, I can watch it Any Time I Want To!* I think. But of course I don't watch the movies any more often when I own them; they just take up more space on the shelf.

I wrote "Property of Jesus Christ, borrowed by Steven James" on the inside flap of the books on my bookshelf. It's supposed to serve as a reminder to me that I don't actually own the books, that I don't own anything, but the words also serve as a pretty good reminder to the people who borrow my books who to return them to. So there's this added benefit thing going on.

❧

I was reading through one of those in-flight magazine catalogs one time when I realized I could call the toll-free number right there on the airplane and order a pop-up hot dog cooker. It looked like a normal toaster except it had hot dog–shaped slots instead of bread-shaped slits. It cooks two at a time and sells for only $49.95.

There was also a heated towel stand for just $199.95 to "take the chill off towels prior to use." Until I read that ad, I'd always thought I was the chilly thing when I got out of the shower, not the towel. *Hmm, I don't want a chilly towel*, I thought. *Maybe I should get one.*

I flipped the page and found a remote-controlled deck umbrella for the low price of $695. If I got one of those, I wouldn't have to wind that pesky crank up and down *ever again*! There was a grill for $995 along with a special grill lamp, "the next best thing to natural sunlight," for $125 . . . a closet shoe rack for thirty-six pairs of shoes . . . and a special hanger that would hold up to twenty pairs of pants. *If I got those*, I thought, *I could get thirty more pairs of shoes and another dozen pair of pants and have room for them all!*

There was a CD shelf that holds a thousand CDs. It looked like it would take up half the living room. I decided against that one. It must have been designed pre-iTunes. Oops. Someone's looking for a new job.

I even found a handmade toad house (yes, it was actually *handmade*) for *only* $24.95, caller ID for your television so you can see who's calling you while you watch the big game, a $1,699.99 Michael Jordan jersey, and a King Tut Life-Sized Sarcophagus Cabinet that would cost $145 just to ship. I won't tell you the total price tag on that one.

All of these things I could have ordered right there on the airplane using my American Express card and the in-flight phone.

I met a pastor once at a coffee shop. "We're a New Testament church," he told me as he explained how his church was better than mine. "We do things the way the early church did."

I was really impressed. "So you don't believe in personal property?"

"Huh?"

"You know, you don't believe in personal ownership but share everything as a community? Like the early church did. Pooling your resources, you know. Like that?"

He looked at me like I was Sean Hannity and he was the head of the Democratic National Convention. "Um, we're not a commune, no."

"Oh."

I thought of saying something like, "So I guess when the early Christians shared everything it was God-honoring, but if we were to do it today we'd be cultists or commies?" but decided that might not be the best way to jump-start our friendship.

I'm in awe of people who own nothing. I read that when some of the nuns who worked with Mother Teresa moved into a home that was carpeted, the first thing they did was remove the carpeting so they'd be better able to identify with the poor. I might have replaced the carpeting, but I doubt I would have removed it.

I'm even blown away by people who live *as if* they owned nothing. People like Bug. Or Mark the monk.

I'm typing this on a laptop computer—*my* laptop computer. In a few minutes I'll be saving this document in the file folder entitled "My Documents."

I almost never use "Shared Documents." I know it's on the computer somewhere, but I'd have to search to find it.

In one of the fabulous mysteries of faith, those who believe in Jesus have actually become part of Jesus. We are, according to the New Testament writers, the body of Christ (see Romans 12:5). It's sort of a mystical thing.

All true believers are part of the body of a God who is a spirit. Maybe Bug is Jesus's earlobe beset with a dangling earring, and Mark is a fingernail, and I'm one of the whiskers on his cheek. Who knows. But all believers are part of Jesus's presence on earth, his body. A body that came to serve, not to be served. That came to think of others first, not itself.

In those rare moments when I begin to unravel the threads of selfishness that seem to be woven so deeply into my character, my priorities, my choices, my goals, and my heart, I begin to see the pathway that leads me farther from myself and closer to the rabbi whose body I'm a vital part of. The more I empty myself of pride, ego, selfishness, greed, the "life-grabbing life," as Jesus put it (I'm paraphrasing, but see Luke 17:33), the more fulfilled my life becomes. The life-grabbers are the life-losers; those who open their lives up to God and to others are the recipients of a truer, freer life. Every moment that I spend on the me-focused life means losing out on the deeper realties of the Jesus-focused life.

"Join the dance," he says.

"What's it gonna cost me?"

"Everything and nothing."

"Oh. Well, I'll have to think about that."

∾

In Proverbs 30:8–9, Agur prayed that God would give him neither poverty nor riches, because riches might lead him to trust in himself and poverty might lead him to steal.

I have a hard time picturing many of my churchgoing friends praying along with Agur, "Lord, please don't make me rich, because it might lead me further from you." Instead they prefer the words of their favorite intercessor, St. Jabez, the Patron Saint of Prosperity, "Increase my territory! Increase my territory!" Pant. Pant. Pant.

In the prayer we call the Lord's Prayer, Jesus taught believers to pray for daily bread (see Matthew 6:11). Daily bread can look like lots of different things, but I don't think it usually looks like your investment portfolio. That sounds like tomorrow's bread to me.

ravens feeding elijah

another raven
lands beside your weathered hand.
food for today.
for now.

another paycheck lands
inside your shiny mailbox.
you reach for it and you rip open the envelope.
and you sigh. it's not much. but it's enough.
for today.
for now.

another black form rises from the sand,
and wings its way up into the crystal clear sky.
until tomorrow.
when it will land again.

providence.

Sometimes it seems like Jesus wants me to be content, and sometimes it seems like he doesn't. On the one hand, he never let his followers settle in or become comfortable on this planet; instead he told them to think about and store up treasures for the life to come. Yet at the same time he inspired them to embrace every moment as a glorious gift without worry or stress or fear about the troubles tomorrow might bring. Or the bread it might not.

"As they were walking along someone said to Jesus, 'I will follow you no matter where you go.' But Jesus replied, 'Foxes have dens to live in, and birds have nests, but I, the Son of Man, have no home of my own, not even a place to lay my head'" (Luke 9:57–58).

"I'll follow you wherever you go," we tell Jesus.

"I have no home," he says. "Will you follow me to the place where you don't either?"

∽

The Quaker author Thomas R. Kelly noted that as God works in our lives, we become less attached to the world and yet, at the same time, more concerned for the world: "He plucks the world out of our hearts, loosening the chains of attachment. And He hurls the world into our hearts, where we and He together carry it in infinitely tender love."[1]

Christians find themselves in the strange business of disentangling themselves from the things of this world while busily engaging themselves more deeply than ever in the affairs of life. God both severs our attachments to heated towel stands and remote-controlled deck umbrellas and at the same time awakens within us a deeper love for those who make and sell and distribute them. Somehow Christians should be both more in love with the world and less in love with the world than anyone else.

The author of the book of Hebrews ties the presence of God together with the idea of contentment: "Keep your lives free from the love of money and be content with what you have, because God has said, 'Never will I leave you; never will I forsake you'" (Hebrews 13:5 NIV).

Loving money won't lead to contentment; only loving God does. The more aware we are of God's presence, the less we'll worry about tomorrow's bread. The less we'll have to fear. And the more peace we'll find today. And so Christianity brings a deep and rich contentment along with a thrilling expectancy. Peace with the world and anticipation of better days to come.

After all, those who find contentment with God are the wealthiest people of all. They can never become poor because no one can ever take away the things they treasure most.

"Sell what you have and give to those in need," said Jesus. "This will store up treasure for you in heaven! . . . Wherever your treasure is, there your heart and thoughts will also be" (Luke 12:33–34). I think that within these words is an invitation for us to ask not only the self-evident question, "Where is my treasure?" but also the much more important question, "Where is my heart?"

Zing.

Here's the challenge—to live every moment with total contentment but without a hint of complacency. To never let envy or ambition or greed steal joy from the deep places of our beings, but to never become self-satisfied by where we are on our journey either. Anxiety is one danger; apathy is the other. Jesus is the answer to both.

> i'm climbing, always climbing
> looking for the next handhold
> hoping to reach the summit
> before dusk.
> and sometimes i think you're asking
> me to let go and fall into the
> moments stretching all around me.
> and sometimes i hear you telling me
> to reach higher than my arms
> could possibly go.
>
> conundrum.

Lots of times in the New Testament, Christians are called aliens, foreigners, and nomads on this planet. This is a very hard lesson to learn: I have more in common with the lost, homeless vagrant on the street corner than the middle-class suburbanite paying off his mortgage. Especially since I am the middle-class suburbanite paying off his mortgage.

Yet according to Jesus, this earth is not our home. This stuff is not my stuff. This backpack is not my backpack. And if I would have bought one of Bug's "I own nothing" T-shirts, it would not be my "I own nothing" shirt.

The problem is that it sure feels like it is. This sure seems like my laptop computer. This sure seems like my home. This house, this yard, that shed, the sound of cars on the nearby highway, the kids shooting baskets up the hill, the birds in the woods behind the house. It all seems so real, so reliable, so permanent.

It sure seems like home to me.

And that's the danger for me—becoming comfortable here. Moving in where I don't belong. Becoming entangled on this side of paradise. It's so hard to live as if heaven is my home when I can make myself so comfortable here with pop-up hot dog cookers and handmade toad houses. Despite myself, I keep trying to move in here over and over again in so many ways.

But yet, I own nothing.

This planet is not my home.

Getting everything I wish for is not the blessing it appears to be.

Zing.

I have to remind myself of these things over and over again.

Foxes have holes, birds have nests, but those who follow the Son have no place to lay their heads. They just have a place to lay their hearts as they pick their way toward home.

— sixteen

faith in doubt

Okay, I admit it, sometimes I do have a hard time believing in God. Not so much his reality. That's not the big problem for me. It's more like his concern. It's like I know he's there, I really do, but I wonder how much of my day-to-day life really matters to him. Does he really care about the details? About my feelings? Do my dreams really matter to God? I find it easier to have faith in the big things than the little ones. And doubts seem to crop up the most when my prayers aren't being answered.

I used to keep a prayer journal in which I'd record the day I prayed for certain things and then the date God answered that prayer. Some of them were answered right away, even before I could finish praying them. Others were answered after weeks and months. And some still have a blank in the answer column, even more than a decade later.

A few years ago I spent several weeks writing and then directing a special Easter program for our church. It had a combination of poetry readings, dramatic sketches, storytelling, and even dance (which we called "devotion in motion" so the elders would be okay with it).

I felt that the service would be great for people who weren't Christians, that they'd be able to really grasp what our story is all about. But when

I invited my neighbors, they all declined. A little too politely. And I started to get mad at God. After all I'd done for him, the least he could do was send a little encouragement my way and answer my prayers about my neighbors. He just wasn't acting according to my agenda or within my time frame.

And that can be very annoying.

∽

There's a lot I don't understand about prayer.

Jesus made one of his most astounding promises concerning prayer. He actually told his followers that if they asked for anything in his name, God would give it to them (see John 14:13–14). Yet—and here's the rub—sometimes God chooses not to. Take Paul, for example. He was definitely the go-to man in God's starting lineup, yet when he prayed to be delivered from spiritual oppression, God told him, "My grace is sufficient for you" (2 Corinthians 12:9 NIV), which is a spiritual way of saying, "Learn to live with it, dude."

Even some of Jesus's prayers went unanswered, which is a bit disconcerting. Christians don't typically admit this, but if you take things at face value, you have to.

He asked his Dad to create such unity among his followers that the world would be convinced of the reality of God's love (see John 17:20–26). I know some scholars say, "Well, you see, Jesus meant *spiritual* unity there," but that's a cop-out if I ever heard one. Believers already have spiritual unity with Jesus and with each other. He didn't need to ask for that. Instead, Jesus specifically asked for a kind of unity that would be visible, attractive, and revelatory to the world, yet when the world looks at Christians today, they all too often see infighting, backstabbing, belittling, and whining instead of overwhelming evidence of Jesus's presence and God's love.

So much for that prayer.

You may also remember Jesus asking God for another pathway through the future that didn't involve the cross, and God told him no. So here's Jesus, the world's greatest believer, the most spiritually attuned person our planet has ever known, and even he didn't get everything he asked God for.

In a weird sort of way, that makes me feel a little better.

Jesus said that if we have faith the size of a mustard seed, we could tell a mountain to get up and walk down the street, but I've never yet seen a mountain moonwalk across town. I don't think anyone has.

> no pope who has ever lived
> no pastor who has ever preached
> no theologian who has ever
> cleared his throat
> has moved even
> the smallest mountain by
> the power of his himalayan prayers.
>
> in all the wide span of the ages
> no believer yet has had faith
> the size of a mustard seed.
> > that makes me feel a little better
> > when i look in the mirror and
> > wonder why my prayers
> > seem so frail and vain.

It'd be easy to believe if every prayer were immediately answered the exact way that we wanted. God would get an A+ in customer satisfaction then for sure. But as it is, I've noticed a rather long line to the heavenly complaint department. And God doesn't seem to be in any big hurry to hire an image consultant to get things turned around.

I know sometimes our prayers remain unanswered because of our lack of faith, or our disobedience, or God's indecipherable plan, or maybe even spiritual forces of darkness. I know all that. But it doesn't always help. I still end up with a lot of questions about how prayer really works and about when (and if) it does any good.

Somehow we're asked to keep believing even when it's hard, even when God is silent, even when he doesn't seem to be listening. And yes, even when he seems to be ignoring us. I wish believers were a little more honest about the whole thing and just admitted that sometimes God doesn't answer our prayers even when we do everything right.

∼

When I think of all this, it brings to my mind the story of the demon-possessed boy (see Mark 9:14–29). The person I can identify with most in the story is the kid's dad.

Now, I'm not saying that my kids are demon-possessed—although I have to admit there have been times when I've wondered just what criteria you have to meet before calling in the friendly neighborhood exorcist.

No, what I relate to is how desperate this guy felt. How he believed but also doubted—at the very same time. That's where I find myself all too often.

This man came to Jesus because he had nowhere else to turn. He'd tried everything, but no one could help his boy. In fact, even Jesus's disciples failed to rescue the son from the dark forces controlling him. So when Jesus arrives, the man begs him, "Please, sir. If there is anything you can do—"

And Jesus interrupts him: "What do you mean *if*? Everything is possible to someone who believes!" His words are both a rebuke and an invitation, laced with fiery, unyielding love.

And here's where I enter the story. Here's where this guy could be me.

"I do believe!" he cries. "Help my unbelief!"

"I do believe!" I cry. "Help my unbelief!"

Even that night before the Easter service I'd worked so much on, I was filled with ifs and doubts and pesky little fears. It wasn't a big, earth-shattering kind of doubting God, just the everyday type of giving up on him because he doesn't seem to be listening or coming through the way you'd expect. From my experience this is a much more common kind of problem than having demon-possessed relatives, although for you it might be different. Depends a little on what family you marry into.

For me, the little nibbling doubts are the kind that seem to populate my heart. And part of my problem is the whole "not my will but yours" thing.

Most of the time if I pray "Your will, not mine" at all, I'm secretly hoping God will give me my way in the end after all—maybe as a reward for praying for his will.

Other times it's a cop-out: "O God, please heal Grandma . . . if it's your will." It's like my way of giving God an easy out because I don't really expect a miracle. I say, "If it's your will!" so that if God doesn't answer my prayer I can still keep believing in him: "Oh well, I guess it just wasn't God's will." It's almost like a way to let him off the hook.

I know it's a pathetic way to pray, but still I find myself doing it sometimes because my doubts just won't go away.

And in that way this guy is like me.

"I do believe!" he cries. "Help my unbelief!"

Faith and doubt both circle through his heart. It isn't faith alone or doubt alone that stands in center ring. They're both there, fighting, feinting, swinging, pounding each other, trying to go for the knockout punch. And sometimes this man can't tell who's winning. He wants faith to win, but with so many failures and disappointments behind him over the years, he's not certain about anything anymore. His faith has gotten pummeled, and now he's reeling beneath the blows of his reality-induced doubts.

"I do believe!" he cries. "Help my unbelief!"

I think this guy's response is one that God readily accepts. After all, God never asks us to deny our doubts or pretend they're not real. He's into honesty. Mostly he just wants us to be up-front with him about what we believe and what we doubt. When we stop pretending, he starts listening.

∿

Here's what I realized just the other night: to doubt is not the same as refusing to believe.

Now, that may not sound all that profound to you, but this realization has really helped me understand Jesus's different responses to the people he encountered. Typically Jesus was patient with genuine seekers but had little tolerance for coldhearted religionists.

All throughout Scripture, God is infuriated by people who are unrepentant, stiff-necked (what a great term!), and stubborn. As Jesus told the Pharisees, "You search the Scriptures because you believe they give you eternal life. But the Scriptures point to me! Yet you refuse to come to me so that I can give you this eternal life!" (John 5:39–40).

This sin of refusing God's love and resisting his agenda seals us off from entering his story. As Jesus told his disciples, "Anyone who believes and is baptized will be saved. But anyone who refuses to believe will be condemned" (Mark 16:16).

Throughout the Old Testament, the Israelites kept hardening their hearts against God, refusing his love over and over again like a bratty little kid pouting in the backseat because his dad won't stop at McDonald's. And eventually, their stubbornness became a deep wedge between them and God—a wedge that could only be removed by God's strange, unfathomable grace.

Yet throughout the Bible we find some people who really did want to walk the road of faith toward God, even if they were pulled down at times by the centripetal force of their doubts.

In the famous story of Jesus walking on the water, Peter showed great faith by joining Jesus on the lake, but then, when Peter saw the raw, unbridled force of the wind, "he was terrified and began to sink. 'Save me, Lord!' he shouted. Instantly Jesus reached out his hand and grabbed him. 'You don't have much faith,' Jesus said. 'Why did you doubt me?'" (Matthew 14:30–31).

See? Peter had some faith and some doubt—enough faith to walk on the water, yet enough doubt to begin to sink. Even that great hero of the faith, Abraham, who "never wavered in believing God's promise" (Romans 4:20) clearly had seasons of doubt (see Genesis 15 for some pretty specific examples). God's greatest heroes of faith are often legendary for their doubts.

Doubts crowd around us. "Save me, Lord!" we yell into the storm. And he grabs us by the hand and lifts us up to stand by his side.

For some people it really is that dramatic—storms and demons threaten their very existence. But more often than not, the things that pound away at my faith aren't nearly that newsworthy. And I don't exactly yell those words. I just kind of whisper them softly in the background of everyday life: "I'm hurting here, God; I'm doubting you again. I don't want to, but I am. Do something. Anything. I'm sinking. Are you there?"

When I was in eighth grade I ran on our junior high school's cross-country team. Our school didn't have a track, so we held practices at a park about a half mile away from campus. I always had a ton of books in my knapsack and nowhere good to store it while we ran (we didn't have lockers), so I just stuck it under this big droopy pine tree at the edge of the park.

Since I'd grown up in a religious home, I knew all about prayers, so every day I would stick my book bag under that tree and ask God to help it be there at the end of practice. And each night it would be there, right where I left it. This went on for a couple weeks until one night I guess I was really mad about something, probably some kids picking on me, and I thought, *I hate you, God! You don't care about me or my stupid backpack or anything. And I'm not gonna pray that it'll be there because it's gonna be there whether or not I talk to you about it anyway. So screw you!*

Those are the kinds of things I thought when I was angry and in the eighth grade. Only my language was a tad more colorful and lively back then.

That night after practice I went to the tree to get my backpack. And of course, as you've already guessed, it was gone.

My books were there, though. Piled neatly under the tree. My pencils and pens were there, my homework was there, slid under the books so the papers wouldn't blow away, but the backpack was gone. I stood there dumbfounded. Why would some kid steal my book bag and take the time to neatly pile my books up under that tree? It might have been a prank by a friend of mine, but no one else knew I put the bag there, and no one else knew what I'd told God that day.

When my dad picked me up, I told him someone had stolen my backpack, and he reported it to the police, but I knew they'd never catch the culprit because God doesn't leave fingerprints at the scene of the crime.

Even though he does leave them on eighth-grade boys.

Like me.

The night before the big Easter production I was sitting in the living room thinking about how God wasn't going to use the event to reach anybody and woe is me because I prayed for my neighbors to come and they didn't want to and how could this happen to me and why hadn't he answered that prayer and so on and so forth, blah, blah, blah. And with every little complaint and doubt, the water was rising.

Then, at 9:45 p.m., there was a knock at the door. I set down the novel I was reading and glanced out the window. *What on earth?*

The knock came again, and I stood up to see who was there.

∽

Of course Jesus always calls us toward a deeper, fuller, richer faith. He never feeds our doubts. And obviously a time must come when the tide turns in favor of faith if a person is going to call himself a *believer*. After all, when Jesus was proving his rising from the dead to Thomas, he invited his friend to feel the evidence for himself: "'Put your finger here; see my hands. Reach out your hand and put it into my side. Stop doubting and believe.' Thomas said to him, 'My Lord and my God!'" (John 20:27–28 NIV).

In that moment, Thomas's faith swung a roundhouse punch and knocked doubt to the mat.

And so on this day when the father of a demon-possessed boy feels helpless and hopeless, he turns to Jesus and says, "The evil spirit often makes him fall into the fire or into water, trying to kill him. Have mercy on us and help us. Do something if you can" (Mark 9:22).

And with a thunderous whisper that is able to unchain a soul or unseat a demon, Jesus says, "What do you mean *if*?"

"I do believe!" cries this man. "Help me overcome my doubts!" There's no resisting Jesus here. No refusal to believe. Just a man ready for the Son to come in. A man done with his ifs.

And in response to his words, Jesus doesn't yell at him, doesn't get on his case, doesn't shake his head or roll his eyes or reach into his back pocket and pull out a set of creeds and say, "Sorry, buddy. You need to agree to every point on this doctrinal statement here or there's nothing I can do for you. I need people on my side who are doctrinally pure."

Instead, Jesus nods. He's used to this. Maybe he puts his hand on the guy's shoulder. Then he helps him. In a miraculous fashion, Jesus frees this man's son from the terrible forces controlling him. "The boy lay there motionless, and he appeared to be dead. A murmur ran through the crowd, 'He's dead.' But Jesus took him by the hand and helped him to his feet, and he stood up" (Mark 9:26–27).

This man had come to Jesus with a little bit of faith and a desire for more, and in his encounter with Jesus, his faith and his son's life were transformed forever.

∽

In his brief, desperate plea this man summarizes my journey of faith: "I do believe you, Jesus. Help my unbelief."

I know my faith is real, but it's also ragged. It's intact but rough around the edges. Some people's faith is clean-shaven and neatly trimmed and smells a little bit like Old Spice aftershave. Other people's faith is all unkempt and hairy and probably has lice. Mine is in-between. It's sort of scruffy, like a five o'clock shadow with a little goatee thing going on.

While God knows the future and all the different ways this frayed world may choose to knot itself up, I believe that the future is being written by the choices of the present. I think our choices have been the major reason Jesus's prayer in John 17 still remains unanswered. Our choices do make a difference. And that includes the choice of whether or not to pray. Because our prayers do tug at the heartstrings of heaven. And for every unanswered scream in the dark is another backpack waiting unceremoniously under the branches of a pine tree night after night.

I love how the author of Hebrews puts it: "Let us come boldly to the throne of our gracious God. There we will receive his mercy, and we will find grace to help us when we need it" (Hebrews 4:16).

gallop into the throne room,
stop all this quivering with uncertainty
and peering through the lattice.
the king will see you now.
but only if you are willing
to see him.

❦

I opened the door and found myself staring into the face of a man I'd never seen before. "Yes?"

"Hi, I'm Rudy," he said. "I used to live in this neighborhood and I know your neighbor Carl, and I've been going to this one church but I'm not going to go there anymore, and I was wondering if you knew of any churches I could go to?"

"You're looking for a church to go to tomorrow?"

"Uh-huh."

"And you just decided to drive up to my house and ask me about it here at almost ten o'clock at night?"

Rudy nodded.

"Um, uh, c'mon in."

I told Rudy about our special Easter service and gave him directions to our church. "Thanks. I really appreciate this," he told me.

"Um, yeah, no problem," I said. He walked back outside and was gone. And that was that.

Now, I know this isn't very impressive as far as miracles go. It's not even close to being in the same league as walking on water or being freed from a demon. Maybe it wasn't even a miracle at all. But it was *something*, and it was big enough to take my hand and pull me back up out of the waters once again. I think that's how most miracles work. We're nudged back toward faith again by momentary glimpses of the divine.

Most of us don't have demon-possessed kids. Most of us aren't sinking into the sea in the middle of a hurricane. Instead we have whiny kids with runny noses, and doubts about whether or not God really cares if we get the new job we've been praying about. But here's what I've learned: no matter how big our doubts and our beliefs are, Jesus accepts them because he accepts us.

Every day I walk through a minefield of confession and confusion, certainty and perplexity, courage and hesitation. I trust the Bible, and yet I question parts of it. I believe in God, yet most of the time he doesn't seem as real to me as I'd like. I trust his promises, yet sometimes I doubt he'll really answer my prayers. I want to honor him, but at times I want to go my own direction instead.

And through it all I'm beginning to realize that the true journey of faith isn't marked by certainty but by a mixture of belief and doubt living together in a refining tension. Some people might call doubt a sin, but I wouldn't. I think faith is the ability to see the truth while it's still invisible, and doubt is the inevitable question that asks for proof of the unknown.

I'm reassured by the promise in Romans 8:26–27 that God's Spirit is praying for me, pleading for me, groaning for me in a language beyond both words and pain. He's on my side, praying to himself for me.

I guess I can relax a little bit knowing that. It kind of takes the pressure off.

I have enough checks in the answer column to know that destinies really are changed when I make my requests of the King. Fate moves over to the passenger seat when I pray. Not always in the ways I want, but always in the ways that are best.

There's so little about God that I understand, so many ways to sink in the waves. "I do believe," I cry over and over again, day after day. "I do believe you, Jesus! Help me overcome my doubts!"

And he nods. He's used to this. He takes my hand and leads me deeper into the reality of who he is over and over again. Day after day. As we move further and further from shore, weaving gracefully between the stars.

— seventeen

the bruise on the skin
of the world

Some people think evil is the opposite of good, but I don't think that's how things work. If it was, evil would be just as powerful as good. The devil would be an equal match for God. This world would have only a 50 percent chance at a happy ending. I don't buy any of that.

Instead, I think evil is the subtle corruption of good. After all, silence isn't the opposite of music; noise is. If you change only a few notes of a song, you distort the whole melody, create dissonance, and turn the harmony into discord. Just a subtle distortion, a slight corruption, is all you need to wreck the whole song. By changing a few notes you change everything.

I think that's how evil works. Not by overpowering good but by corrupting it one note at a time: quietly turning self-confidence into pride, physical attraction into lust, pleasure into indulgence, respect into envy, self-preservation into selfishness, ambition into greed. It's not the opposite of good but the tainting of it.

It's like an apple whose skin is bruised. At its core, the apple is still good, but it isn't wholly good anymore. Evil is the bruise on the skin of the world.

I believe that early on in our story, God dreamed, spoke, shaped, created a good planet in a good universe. And he fashioned one special species in his own special image, bringing them to life by breathing (literally, *inspiring*) his Spirit into them. But evil crept in. The snake slithered onto the scene. And ever since then, the bruise has continued to spread.

Suffering is always just around the bend on this unexplainable, inexplicable, agathokakological planet. And more often than not, evil is flexing its muscles somewhere in view of my life.

And yet, through it all, Christians have the audacity to claim that God is still in control, that he is overwhelmingly full of love, and that—despite the evil that we can see all too clearly in the world around us—we should pin our hopes on this God who seems awfully hidden indeed.

As St. Teresa of Avila considered how hidden her Lord remained from her, she prayed this startlingly honest prayer:

> It is my belief, O Lord,
> that if I could hide from you
> as you hide from me,
> your love for me would not tolerate it:
> indeed, you are always with me
> and have me always in your sight.
> No, this is intolerable, my Lord.
> I beg you to consider how insulting it is
> to one who loves you so much.[1]

When I first started working on this book, my neighbor Florence was dying. Her husband, Carl, had been married to her for fifty-four years and was taking care of her at home. She'd just come back from her latest trip to the hospital, and I was on our back deck writing when Carl came outside and waved to me. I stopped typing and joined him. "How's Florence?" I asked.

"Not good." Carl's face was a storm of pain and loss—a flurry of questions I couldn't even begin to fathom. "She's not gonna be with us much longer."

Then he tells me about her trips to the hospital, and her failed kidneys, and how last weekend she wandered out of the house screaming, and how she woke him up at 3:00 this morning asking if her mother was going to cook their breakfast. "Honey, your mother has been dead for fifty years," he had to tell her.

And I don't say anything. I don't know what to say. He talks for a while about the costs of insurance and her hospital stays and the injustice of it all ("Her last stay cost over $150,000 . . . how can they do that to people?") and how he needs a new roof and those neighbors down the block, did anyone ever move into their house?

And then he pauses and stares past me toward the mountains, and he shakes his head. "Don't ever grow old," he says.

And I say, "Beats the alternative."

Then Carl smiles and laughs in his good ol' boy eastern Tennessee way, and then we talk a little about how none of us gets out of this alive and how our only hope is for a better place.

"Without the good Lord," says Carl, who hasn't gone to church in decades, "we wouldn't have nuthin', would we? We'd be just a grain of sand in the water. We'd be nuthin', wouldn't we?" Carl is one of the best non-churchgoing theologians I've ever met.

I nod and agree that without God we wouldn't have much hope at all.

And then Carl says, "But sometimes you gotta wonder why God is punishing her . . . why he's letting this happen when she never hurt no one. . . . You gotta wonder about that sometimes."

Carl stops looking at the mountains then, and he looks at me for an answer. He knows I write Christian books. He knows I speak at churches. He expects me to have an answer. And I say something about how even Jesus wondered about suffering. About how even Jesus knew what it was like to feel abandoned by God and to feel alone in a pain-filled and painful world. And I'm not really sure it helps Carl feel any better. I know there's some truth to it all, but it sounds shallow and trite. I don't want it to, but it does. And I'm not even sure I believe it myself. I know I'm supposed to believe it, but I have some of the same questions Carl has. I'm embarrassed by how few answers I have. I wish the pope or Rick Warren or maybe Bono would step out of the bushes and explain it all to us, but they don't, and then Florence wakes up and yells something indistinguishable from within the brick walls of their home, and Carl turns to the door.

"She's gettin' sick again," he says. "I gotta go be with her."

And I say, "Yeah, I'll talk with you later."

"Okay," says Carl, and he goes inside to be with his dying wife, and I go back home to write a book about God.

dead wasps in the windowsill.
yesterday i watched them
trying to fly through the glass.
today they lie still in death. all their
hopes sheathed in their dry, quiet bodies.
  all their busy buzzings are over
now that they're dead
and forgotten on this side
of the glass.

I suppose if God has an Achilles heel, it's this question of pain. I mean, couldn't God have done a better job of designing this planet? Couldn't he have made a world without dying spouses and failed kidneys and faltering minds and six-figure hospital bills? A world without suicide bombers and rapists and child-abusing priests?

Where is God in the midst of it all? Where is God in the concentration camps and the roadside bombs, the car accidents and the brain tumors, the hate crimes and the genocide? Where is he? Why is he so silent? Is he punishing us? Neglecting us? Is he out to get us? Couldn't he have found a way to quench the insatiable appetite for evil this world seems to have?

I don't really know the answer. Part of me wants to say, "He did create a world without all that stuff, but then we had to go and screw the whole thing up." And I know there's some truth to that, but it doesn't seem like a very satisfying answer. If anything, it's not a complete one.

I know some of the common answers people have given over the centuries, but they don't always help much, either. Too often they make God seem either heartless or impotent.

"He has a bigger plan in mind," we say. "And sometimes he uses pain to teach us lessons!" Well, I can think of better ways to make a point than AIDS and starving orphans. And most of my non-Christian friends can too.

"He doesn't always approve of everything he allows," we say. "Sometimes he lets people do things he doesn't approve of." Well, he lets kids get abused every day, and a good dad would never let his daughter get molested, no matter what—not if he had the power to stop it. So either God doesn't care or he's not strong enough to intervene.

"Well, he allows us to make choices," we reply. "You wouldn't want to be a robot, would you?" Of course not, but love always sets limits. I limit where my children can play because I love them. I don't let them play checkers on the interstate. Total freedom isn't love; it's neglect. Or abuse. God should rein in our freedoms if he really loves us. And besides, what about earthquakes or tsunamis or birth defects? We don't choose those.

It's like each answer is a caricature of the real answer, and like all caricatures, they each have a little bit of truth to them, but they're cartoonish if taken by themselves. They resemble the right answer but contain only facets of it.

The best book I've read on the question of pain is Peter Kreeft's slim offering *Making Sense of Suffering*. I think he has the right approach. "I do not claim to serve up the total answer to this deep and painful problem," he writes, "but to assemble clues, which are only facets of the answer, like the facets of a diamond. No one can see all the facets of a diamond at once; our angle of vision always limits us. But we can see things of light and beauty. We see these in the middle of great darkness, as we find diamonds far underground. We can hope to find light in the darkness of suffering, too."[2]

At times I see those lights in our world, shimmers of glory on the edge of suffering, blessings that come so very cleverly disguised, a good core deep beneath the bruise. Horror and hope vie for my attention and allegiance almost every day.

And of course I know that my perspective is limited. I can't begin to see all the angles at once. "How could evil exist?" we ask when we see one side of the coin.

"How could God not?" we ask when we see the other.

mary jo's baptism

mary jo is six years old and
she is dying of a brain tumor.
in two weeks they will operate.
again.
and today at church, she's being baptized.

she wants to do it. she asked to be baptized today,
before the surgery.
so she stands in front of the only congregation
she has ever known
and answers the pastor's questions.

do you know you have sinned
and cannot get into heaven on your own?
yes.

do you trust in jesus to take away your sins?
yes. (and this time she nods and smiles, too.)

why do you want to be baptized today?
'cause i love jesus and want people to know it!

and he smiles and she smiles and the congregation smiles.
though a few people cry.

her daddy baptizes her. and as he
tips her beneath the water, the congregation's
heart beats as one.
and she is baptized in the name of the father
    and the son
    and the holy spirit.

now her daddy is crying, too.
and then mary jo, the six-year-old girl
with curls and cute chubby hands
and a brain tumor
stands up with dripping wet clothes
and she looks the size of a mountain.

we applaud
and a smile leaps from her teeth and comforts us all,
as sunlight climbs into the room to watch.
and when it's over, the sunlight decides to stay in this baptist church.
forever.

                        ᔕ

Every one of us has met a Mary Jo—a quiet reminder that there is still hope for the world. A glimmer of light as God tips the prism once again.

Some people believe that God is the author of pain; others say he just allows it. On the one hand, I can see how some people say he's responsible for it since he is in charge of the universe, but on the other hand, I can also see how it's easy to make him the scapegoat.

I remember pushing my daughter Trinity on the swing out behind our house. She was six at the time, and I was messing around with her, pushing her really high and then swinging her from side to side. Getting a little out of hand. Just being a dad.

Finally I got carried away and pushed her sideways toward the tree to make it As Exciting As Humanly Possible, and she smacked into the tree at full swing velocity. There was this sickening crunch and then a wail that enveloped the whole neighborhood.

I ran over to her, and she jumped into my arms. I told her how sorry I was, and between sobs she told me she forgave me as she buried her face in my shoulder. (Don't worry, we're still friends, and I don't think there was any permanent damage, although she does like to remind me of that incident every once in a while, like when she wants a kitten or something.)

I know that every analogy breaks down somewhere, but here goes: although some people might argue that God *is* in the business of slamming us into trees, I don't think he is. My only point with this story is that every time we're wounded in this brutal and beautiful world, we have a choice of which direction to turn. We can run toward our Father or away from him.

My daughter ran to me because she loved me more than she hated me. You only run to the arms of the one who has hurt you if you love him more than you hate your pain.

So does God only allow pain or somehow engineer it? You'll need to come to your own conclusion. This much I do know: if you're more in love with the idea of being wounded than with the hope of being healed, you'll stay away from your Father's arms. If you feel like the whole world owes you a favor, then you won't run to the arms of the one who hurts you. You'll curse him instead.

And there's trust involved in all this too. Do you trust your Daddy's hands on your back, or do you think he's aiming you at the tree with an evil smirk on his face? We both know that only one of those two kinds of dads could ever make the cut to be first-team All God.

∾

In Colossians 1:24 Paul makes the puzzling statement that he was completing the sufferings of Christ: "I fill up in my flesh what is still lacking in regard to Christ's afflictions" (NIV).

What an odd thing to say, especially since Jesus declared on the cross, "It is finished" (John 19:30). Evidently, Paul had come to believe that in a mystical way he was fulfilling that which is already complete, that experiencing suffering is a way to identify with Jesus in his death. Another time he put it this way: "Through suffering, these bodies of ours constantly share in the death of Jesus so that the life of Jesus may also be seen in our bodies" (2 Corinthians 4:10).

We complete that which is already accomplished. And in a deep and real way, this connection with Jesus on the level of pain is part of the privilege of belief: "For you have been given not only the privilege of trusting in Christ but also the privilege of suffering for him" (Philippians 1:29). Of course, this isn't one of the privileges of faith pastors typically highlight in their sermons on Friendship Sunday, but there it is in black and white in the Bible.

All throughout the New Testament, the writers repeatedly emphasize that we're drawn closer to Christ through pain than through pleasure. Crosses and trials and struggles and perseverance lead us deeper into the Father's arms. Most of us tend to aim the trajectory of our lives toward comfort, but that road rarely takes us closer to Christ. Pain is part of the cost of faith. As oddly shaped as it may be, this pain-connection with Jesus is a pivotal piece of the puzzle.

A few years ago my daughters and I attended a ballet with Dana, a good friend of the family and a ballet dancer herself. The girls rushed to the front of the auditorium to sit in the very first row, but Dana said, "No, girls, let's move back. You can't see their feet from there."

Huh. I never would have thought of that. I needed a dancer along, someone who knew what to look for, to point out to me that to fully enjoy the dance, I had to sit back far enough to see the footwork of the dancers.

Things are not always as they appear. If I set a coin on the table, I can only see one side of it at a time. But if I start it spinning on its edge, I can see both sides flash past me at once. The coin looks like a sphere then, but it's just my eyes playing tricks on me. I'm still only seeing one side of the coin at a time, but because the coin is spinning so fast, it doesn't look so one-dimensional anymore.

When it comes to asking God these questions, I have to remind myself that from where I'm seated, I can't always see his footwork.

Sometimes the coin is spinning so fast, I'm not even sure it's a coin anymore.

> twirling toward tomorrow.
>   spinning within today.
> a shadow rises above me
>   that keeps the light at bay.
> the prick of the needle is painful,
>   the deeper it pierces my skin.
> so i take my seat in this moment
>   and wait for the dance to begin.

Paul faced many more problems and difficulties than I ever will. He was imprisoned, whipped repeatedly, beaten, stoned (the almost dying kind, not the frat party kind), left adrift at sea, and faced robbers, riots, hunger, and hypothermia, and yet he was able to claim that our present sufferings aren't worth comparing to the glory that will be given to us in heaven (see Romans 8:18). "So we don't look at the troubles we can see right now," he wrote, "rather, we look forward to what we have not yet seen. For the troubles we see will soon be over, but the joys to come will last forever" (2 Corinthians 4:18).

Sometimes I just need to stop trying to figure God out and move to another seat in the auditorium—one that's not so close to my pain.

That's what Peter did. In his letter to the believers who were being persecuted for their faith, he wrote, "Dear friends, don't be surprised at the fiery trials you are going through, as if something strange were happening to you" (1 Peter 4:12).

It strikes me that he says "as if." Apparently, we should *expect* to suffer. And really, it makes sense that in a world where people have chosen to go their own way rather than God's, there will inevitably be pain, suffering, and dissatisfaction.

The troubles I'm facing right now aren't strange; they're the norm. Why am I so surprised? Tragedy is a given in this sin-stained world. Pain is the default setting for this planet. The reason I get frustrated is that I forget that.

After all, I haven't reached the happy ending yet. I'm still traveling through the land where the witch lives and the curse lingers and children need braces and toasters explode and the checkbook doesn't always balance. All of these things are givens. Most of my frustrations come from my unrealistic expectations about life on this planet.

I admit that sometimes I try to make sense of the suffering in the world by looking for God's ulterior motive: "Maybe he let this happen so that . . ." And if I can't find a good reason, I blame him for being cruel, or at least for being too secretive about his reasons.

That's what Job did. He reached out for God, he called out to God, yet God remained silent. Through all of Job's pleadings and questions and wonderings, God remained silent. Job searched his soul to see if there was some dark, secret sin he'd done that was causing the distance he felt between himself and the Almighty. But he found none. He begged for a hearing before God. He refuted the shallow advice and subtle accusations of his smug friends, and still he suffered, and still God remained silent.

Until God saw that the time was right. And then, when the Almighty spoke to him, Job was humbled into stunned silence: "Then Job replied to the LORD, 'I am nothing—how could I ever find the answers? I will put my hand over my mouth in silence. I have said too much already. I have nothing more to say'" (Job 40:3–5). More than once I've had to place my hand over my mouth, and I can tell you, it isn't a very fun place to be. Especially when it's in a conversation with God.

I guess the more I think about it, the more I doubt that God is the author of our pain. After all, the farmer doesn't go around bruising his own apples. Only his competition would do that.

> Here is another story Jesus told: "The Kingdom of Heaven is like a farmer who planted good seed in his field. But that night as everyone slept, his enemy came and planted weeds among the wheat. When the crop began to grow and produce grain, the weeds also grew. The farmer's servants came and told him, 'Sir, the field where you planted that good seed is full of weeds!'
>
> "'An enemy has done it!' the farmer exclaimed.

"'Shall we pull out the weeds?' they asked.

"He replied, 'No, you'll hurt the wheat if you do. Let both grow together until the harvest. Then I will tell the harvesters to sort out the weeds and burn them and to put the wheat in the barn.'" . . .

Then, leaving the crowds outside, Jesus went into the house. His disciples said, "Please explain the story of the weeds in the field."

"All right," he said. "I, the Son of Man, am the farmer who plants the good seed. The field is the world, and the good seed represents the people of the Kingdom. The weeds are the people who belong to the evil one. The enemy who planted the weeds among the wheat is the Devil. The harvest is the end of the world, and the harvesters are the angels.

"Just as the weeds are separated out and burned, so it will be at the end of the world. I, the Son of Man, will send my angels, and they will remove from my Kingdom everything that causes sin and all who do evil, and they will throw them into the furnace and burn them. There will be weeping and gnashing of teeth. Then the godly will shine like the sun in their Father's Kingdom. Anyone who is willing to hear should listen and understand!"

Matthew 13:24–30, 36–43

"Why is there evil in the world?" Well, the devil is busy bruising God's produce.

"Then why doesn't God just stop him?" One day he will. He'll remove "everything that causes sin and all who do evil" (Matthew 13:41). But for now he's actually allowing the weeds *for the good of the wheat*. It would hurt the wheat too much if he were to pull out the weeds before harvest time. Until then, the roots of the Kingdom-dwellers intertwine with the roots of the Basement-dwellers. Until then, both will grow stronger. But the harvest is coming. And the bruised apples that refuse to be healed will be thrown into the place none of us wants to go.

Once when I was walking through a dark time in my life, I decided to try to deal with my pain logically. Here's what I came up with:

If God is really God, he's in control.
If he's in control, there are no such things as coincidences.
If there are no such things as coincidences, then even these bad experiences can be woven into the fabric of the universe to create something good.

If God is really God, he loves me.
If he loves me, he desires what's best for me.
If he desires what's best for me, he'll allow whatever he needs to in my life to make sure that I'm drawn closer to him.

It was all very sensible and logical. I kept reading and rereading those words, thinking, *Okay, then why the heck don't I feel any better?*

I think it's because even when we have an answer or an explanation, it isn't enough. It'll never be enough because it isn't our reason that's suffering; it's our souls.

Pain isn't a premise to be argued. That's why God didn't send us a syllogism, but a Savior—one who stepped into the center of our pain and allowed the wounds of the world to be poured into his own heart. God's love is greater than our pain. His grace is deeper than our heartache. And he knows firsthand how hard life on this earth can be.

Whatever his reason for allowing suffering, God understands what we're going through and can intimately identify with our questions. He experienced the worst world had to offer, and now he offers to heal the bruises on our souls with time and grace and glimpses of his love.

Is this the final answer to why we suffer? Hardly. I don't pretend that it is. But God never auditioned for the role of Answer Giver of the Universe because most of the time it's not even answers that we want. We want the pain to stop. Or we want a reason big enough to believe in to help us persevere through the tough times. Or we want a companion by our side to maneuver with us through the potholes of life.

So in the end, I'm left with three choices: (1) I can give up on God and tell my heart that he doesn't exist, that he couldn't possibly exist, that life really is as senseless, random, and pointless as it so often appears. (2) I can believe that God does exist but is either too impotent (powerless) to stop the suffering, unaware of the suffering (foolish), unconcerned about those of us who suffer (apathetic), or just plain out to get me (malevolent). None of these kinds of Gods would be worthy of my worship or my life.[3]

Or, (3), I can cling to the belief that God really is in control, and really does love me, and really does work good out of both the joys and the hardships, the rights and the wrongs of this world. I can keep leaning on the invisible arm that has supported me in the past and trust that the one who can shape a star on the tip of his tongue can also shape blessings out of my pain.

Logic only leads me to the place of making a decision: will I believe more in my circumstances or lean more on his love?

In some Christian circles the following verse is used as a cure-all for anything, but the truth that lives in these words is truly powerful and soul-altering: "We know that God causes everything to work together for the good of those who love God and are called according to his purpose for them" (Romans 8:28). I believe that God can take each of our choices and weave them together into a beautiful symphony. Even those choices that are notes out of tune can be orchestrated in his hands into something beautiful. But the score is still being written and the final concert has not yet begun.

I can see the tree looming ahead of me. Regardless of who pushed me so hard, where will I turn when I smack into its trunk?

The teacher told his disciples the tale of a loving shepherd. "Sometimes love wounds those she loves the most," he said. "When a lamb won't stop wandering away, the shepherd breaks her leg so she can't walk far from his side. And so, he protects her by hurting her and he rescues her from herself by sending her a suffering most kind."

And the students nodded.

"But who in the story are you?" he asked them. "The shepherd or the sheep?"

And some said one thing and others said another.

Finally, the teacher said, "We are both the shepherd and the sheep, but we do not wish to be either."

And one of the students in the back of the room added, "So is God. But he is willing to be both."

Then the master handed his staff to that student and sat at her feet, as a child sits before his mother.

Without God's story at the center of the puzzle, without the overarching narrative of harmony, rebellion, sacrifice, and eventual restoration, we will never be able to make sense of the pain and glory of life.

Hints of his love glimmer in the darkness. The heads of wheat sway in the breeze. A girl sings in the candlelight. A father baptizes his daughter. A lamb cries out from a wooden cross. A man takes the hand of his dying wife. A deity weeps 107 times a minute. A king dances along a golden street singing my name.

I am nothing—how could I ever find the answers? I will put my hand over my mouth in silence. I have said too much already. I have nothing more to say.

innocent by association

Andy was the skinniest freshman in the history of my high school. He was so thin and scrawny that he could slide his arm up inside the candy machine in the student union, all the way up to his shoulder, and pluck candy bars from inside. I don't know how he did it. It wasn't supposed to be possible, but it was possible for Andy. It was pretty amazing to watch.

The first time I saw him do it, I thought his arm was gonna get stuck and they'd have to surgically remove the vending machine from his body. I wondered how they'd even fit it inside an ambulance, especially with him attached. I pictured a bunch of paramedics trying to hoist it onto a gurney and wheeling the snack machine and Andy out to the ambulance. Those are the kinds of things I thought about as a teenager. I was not a very stable kid.

Every couple of days we'd gather around the candy machine in the student union—Jason, Brendan, Mark, and me. Andy would lean up against the glass, pull up his shirtsleeve, and slide his arm up into the guts of the machine. Sometimes we had to tip the machine a little bit and shake it for him. That was always dicey, because if one of those things were to fall on you, it wouldn't be pretty. Especially if your arm was stuck inside it when it did.

But the machine never did fall, and pretty soon Andy's hand would emerge clutching a candy bar. "Way to go, Andy!" we'd yell. And he'd hand the candy bar to one of us and stick his hand back in there. He could only do one bar at a time, so we all had to wait our turn. It would take about twenty minutes in all.

We looked at it the same as if the machine had malfunctioned and accidentally given us free candy bars. And it was *sort of* a malfunction since it wasn't keeping out his arm. At least that's how we saw it.

But one day, somehow, the school administration found out. They called us into the office one at a time, like in those cop shows when they interrogate you separate from your friends so you never know who snitched on whom.

I had no idea what they were going to talk to me about when they called me, but then the principal held up a Snickers wrapper, and I knew.

"But we weren't really stealing!" I said.

"The candy bars didn't belong to you. Right?"

"Well—"

"And you didn't pay for them, did you?" He waved the evidence of my crime in front of me.

"It's Andy's fault. He's the one who stole 'em."

"You all did."

"But what if we'd found 'em on the street? Would it have been stealing then, huh?" I know it was a stupid thing to say, but usually when I get caught doing something wrong, my brain shuts down. I've seen the same thing happen to other people too. It seems like a pretty universal human reaction.

"They weren't on the street," the principal said, his tone getting harsher, his face getting redder. "They were in the machine! Did you or didn't you eat any of the candy bars from the machine?"

"Um, yeah, a few," I admitted.

"Did you pay for them?"

"Well, not exactly."

"Then you have to pay for them now." He held out his hand for the money and then added ominously, "And this is going on your permanent record."

So I handed him $3.00 and went home wondering how permanent a permanent record really is. Like, what if I ever wanted to apply to the CIA someday? Would they take one look at my permanent record and see that in the tenth grade I'd eaten some stolen merchandise and deny my application to be a secret agent, all because of Andy's skinny arm?

Or maybe someone would write up this whole thing in the local newspaper, and from that day forward people would look at me differently. Mothers would roll up their car windows when I walked past or shoo their kids back into the house so they wouldn't be exposed to my bad influence and grow up to become a burden on society like me. Things like that.

That night I asked my dad, "At what point is your permanent record wiped clean?"

"Never. That's why it's called permanent."

"Oh."

"Why?"

"Never mind. Um, could I borrow three bucks?"

∾

Here's what I've been asking myself lately: do I want to be known by God, or hidden from him? What do I desire more—total transparency with God, or maybe total immunity from him? Do I really want to see myself as God sees me, or would I rather that he see me as I see me? Do I really want to see the unvarnished version of my life, or maybe keep believing the comfortable illusion that I'm really not so bad after all?

In Hans Christian Andersen's classic tale of "The Emperor's New Clothes," everyone pretends that the king isn't naked until a little boy starts giggling. Only then do the people start laughing at their ridiculous monarch walking naked down Main Street.

Jesus in a manger is God's way of laughing at a world that's busy acting mature. We're parading around, pretending our souls are outfitted with Armani suits, while the whole time we're standing stark naked in the street. We hope maybe God will play along with the charade, but then Jesus points at us from the manger and giggles once again.

We all have undercurrents of regret and remorse running through our lives. Sometimes they come up for air, but usually only a moral meltdown, a personal crisis, or maybe getting caught with our hand in the cookie jar (or the snack machine) brings them to the surface.

Yet unless we get caught, we rarely change direction—stubborn little beings that we are.

Coming to God as is, with all our heartaches and baggage and messy mistakes, is very troubling. So we avoid it. Sometimes because of pride or fear or reputation or who knows what else. We always have our reasons for hanging on to our facades. We're full of reasons. But when we finally step into this glistening christening called Christianity, God both shows us our nakedness and then clothes us with his royal robes from the innermost room of the palace.

When we finally venture our initial "yes" to him, we hear, at last, the "yes" he's been shouting through the cosmos since before the world began.

light washes over my confession
cleansing every prayer with
a lover's caress, the finger-light
touch of a prostitute's hands as she
wipes her tears from a carpenter's feet,
or the carpenter's hands caressing the
feet of a prostitute.

> it's hard to tell which seat i'm in—
> if i'm weeping at his feet,
or if he's weeping at mine.

I think guilt is a powerful argument for God. Without someone to whom we're ultimately held accountable, why would we feel remorse over things we've done, which in most cases are only done to protect ourselves?

What I mean is this: why would an animal feel remorse after doing things that serve its best interests unless it knew somewhere deep inside that pursuing self-interest wasn't in its own self-interest? Unless, of course, it wasn't just an animal.

Regret, I can understand without God. After all, regret is almost always just another form of self-love—we're sorry because we got caught stealing the candy bars and now we have to face the music. But remorse is different. Remorse is sorrow because of the wrong, not because of the consequences of getting caught. True remorse acknowledges something above itself to which it must answer. In a very real way, guilt is an arrow pointing to God.

Humans are thinking animals, reasoning animals, planning, hoping, dreaming, doubting, believing, questioning, and *guilty* animals. To even think about right and wrong in terms of animals seems odd. When one snake kills another snake, it doesn't slither around in remorse. Why should it? And it doesn't seem immoral for the dog to poop in the living room; it's just an inconvenience for me. And even though it's annoying when rabbits eat the lettuce in the garden, they're not stealing. After all, they're just doing what comes natural to them, acting according to their nature.

But for people it's different. This is one thing I think the animal rights advocates miss. They don't get upset when one animal needlessly kills or eats another, only when humans do. But why not? Why do animals only have rights in relationship to us and not to each other, especially if humans are only animals? Don't get me wrong. I'm not saying we should be cruel to animals. I'm just saying that the simple fact that we know we should be kind to animals proves that we're more than animals.

Humans can discern right from wrong, good from evil. We're the only creatures who can actually choose evil, and do. We're the only beings in the universe (that I'm aware of) who know right from wrong and *like doing what's wrong*. We know we should do the right thing, but we don't do it.

Even though we know the rules, we still steal the candy bars.

That's the thing.

Tigers act like tigers. Trees act like trees. Mountains act like mountains. Lions don't act un-liony. Gorillas don't act like donkeys.

In all of creation, only humans don't do what they should, what they were designed to do or intended for. And even when we try our hardest, we still mess things up. We still kick over the diaper pail. We still have messy episodes of failing love.

The apostle Paul explained it like this in Romans 7: "No matter which way I turn, I can't make myself do right. I want to, but I can't. When I want to do good, I don't. And when I try not to do wrong, I do it anyway" (vv. 18–19) and "I don't understand myself at all, for I really want to do what is right, but I don't do it. Instead, I do the very thing I hate" (v. 15).

We're aware of right and wrong—how to act human and inhumane—and all too often choose the latter. And it's true for all of us despite our education level, effort, self-control, and family background.

Only one human being has ever acted the way all humans were intended to act. And we put him to death for it.

∽

My friend Joe Springer (everyone calls him Spring) was looking for a new church. He would go up to the pastors of the churches he was visiting and say, "No church is perfect."

And the pastor would nod and agree, "That's right."

Then Spring would say, "So, before I join yours, tell me what's wrong with it."

At that point the pastors usually remembered something else they had to do and reluctantly offered Spring their heartfelt good-bye along with their sincere hope that he'd join them on Sunday. We're all good at pointing out what's wrong in someone else's church or family or personal life, but when it comes to admitting our own imperfections—well, that's something we'd rather not do.

"It wasn't really stealing— and besides, it was all Andy's fault. He's the one who took the candy bars."

"Who, me? No, God, it was this woman you stuck here in the garden with me. She's the one who made me do it."

I've discovered that if I'm ever going to find the gateway to the kingdom, I have to look in the mirror and see how naked my soul really is.

And when forgiveness arrives, the enigma begins. Because that's when the God who knows everything somehow forgets my mishaps, blunders, misdeeds, and crazy wild pitches. He knows all, yet forgets my sin (see Hebrews 8:12).

Believers in Jesus enter the paradox of becoming wholly who we are. We are complete and being completed. We are saved and being saved. We are pure and being purified. We are perfect and being perfected. We are clean and being cleansed. We don't stop being human— of course not. Instead, we finally begin to experience the deepest realms and the highest heights of what being human is all about. "Who will deliver me from this death-bound body?" asked Paul. "Thank God for Jesus—my only hope of rescue!" (see Romans 7:24–25).

When God led the Israelites out of slavery, he told them, "I have lifted the yoke of slavery from your neck so you can walk free with your heads held high" (Leviticus 26:13). He does the same with those he frees from the slavery of guilt and the pain of the past. Forgiveness lifts the weight of a shame-laden heart and helps me stand once again with my head held high.

And I've been learning recently that God forgives me not only for the wrongs I've done but for wanting to keep doing them. That's where grace really hits home—when my will wants to wander, and I know it, and he knows it, and yet he still loves me. This is a love, a forgiveness, a welcoming I can't even begin to understand. Grace like that can really shake you up.

Some Christians believe that if you sin enough and don't ask for forgiveness each time, you'll get thrown into the big bonfire. Others teach that once you become a believer your soul becomes Teflon coated—no matter what happens, you're fireproof forever. Sin just doesn't stick to you anymore, and you never really need to ask for forgiveness again since God has already forgiven all of your sins past, present, and future.

I think both views miss the whole point. One makes me scared of God—what if I say too many bad words to a chainsaw? What if I'm a little too greedy for that pop-up hot dog cooker? Or what if I have a really rotten day and decide to just give up on Jesus? Can I really lose my inheritance that easily? That's a religion of fear, not love.

But the other view takes God for granted and doesn't seem to prioritize Jesus's calls to true discipleship and obedience highly enough. I've actually heard one of the advocates of this view say, "Once you're saved, you're stuck. No matter what you do, you're gonna end up in heaven." The Bible never talks like that.

So what's the answer? Jesus said that no one can snatch his followers out of his hand, but can we jump?

I've noticed two truths woven throughout the fabric of the Bible. First, once we've ventured our yes to God, we need never doubt his love. He is faithful. He keeps his promises. Nothing can separate us from his love. Nothing. So that's the assurance part.

On the other hand, only those who persevere get to go home to the party at the palace. Cautions against falling away appear all throughout the New Testament. I know Christians interpret some of these verses in different ways, but there's no question the New Testament writers urge us to be wary of sin and its lasting consequences. That's the warning part.

I think God wants me to be both relaxed and wary, secure but not presumptuous. That's the paradox part.

> the raw-boned parable
> takes hold of me again.
> the lamb is the shepherd,
> the shepherd the lamb.
> the one who weeps is the one
> who dies. mourner and savior,
> child and man, God with a beard.
> i'm caught like a splinter in the
> hand of God. and yet he refuses
> to remove me from his
> skin-covered
> tale.

Once when I was going through a really rough time in my life and I told some of my Christian friends what had happened, they were very quick to inform me about how wrong I'd been and how badly I needed to repent. The problem was, I was already well aware of my failings. So the more they preached at me, the more I felt like a worm looking up at their boot heels. Then my friend David said, "Steve, you need to stop feeling so guilty. Guilt might keep you from doing what's wrong, but it'll never lead you to do what's right. Stop trying so hard and surrender to God. Lean on his grace."

It was like I could breathe again. His words were a door swinging open to let the light back into my soul.

Most of the people I meet don't have any trouble feeling guilty. Most of us don't need to be reminded about how often we fail. Instead, most of us need to hear that God really does love us with an everlasting love, that joy really is possible again. That hope really is real. And that nothing can diminish God's love, not even our failures and flub-ups.

Jesus didn't come to kick people when they were down but to help us get back on our feet again when we fail or fall. And we all fail. We all fall. Jesus gives a warning to those who think they have heaven all wrapped up no matter what, but he also offers hope to those crushed by guilt.

Can anything ever separate us from Christ's love? Does it mean he no longer loves us if we have trouble or calamity, or are persecuted, or are hungry or cold or in danger or threatened with death? (Even the Scriptures say, "For your sake we are killed every day; we are being slaughtered like sheep.") No, despite all these things, overwhelming victory is ours through Christ, who loved us.

And I am convinced that nothing can ever separate us from his love. Death can't, and life can't. The angels can't, and the demons can't. Our fears for today, our worries about tomorrow, and even the powers of hell can't keep God's love away. Whether we are high above the sky or in the deepest ocean, nothing in all creation will ever be able to separate us from the love of God that is revealed in Christ Jesus our Lord.

Romans 8:35–39

sailing between the stars

Nothing can separate us from his love. Depression can't. Divorce can't. Bankruptcy can't. Getting caught stealing candy bars can't. Slander and betrayal and shame can't. Not even spilling Joy on the front of your pants. "Despite all these things, overwhelming victory is ours through Christ, who loved us" (Romans 8:37). His love has already overcome the world. It's more powerful than even my doubts. That's my kind of hope. That's real-world grace.

∽

One last thing. You had to know this was coming. After all, any time someone starts talking about forgiveness and "being saved," you have to expect him to mention what happens to those who might be unforgiven or unsaved.

Yes, it is time to talk about the blazing, raging fires of hell.

I've noticed more discussion about hell in recent years, which might be a good sign or a bad one. I don't know. It seems these days that a number of people, many of them influential voices in the Christian community, are questioning the existence of hell. "If God is a God of grace," they say, "how could he send people to hell to be tortured forever?"

Honestly, I think it's a pretty good question, but after reading their stuff, it seems to me like they're ready to jettison the teaching of hell not because of what Jesus had to say about it, but because (a) it doesn't seem logical to them or (b) it doesn't seem to play well with their target audience.

"So how's hell polling these days, Abner?"

"Not so good, Reverend. I think we'd better revise the language. People don't like the idea of eternal condemnation."

"Hmm, yes. I've noticed."

"Maybe we could say something like, 'An unpleasant stay for a pretty long time.' That seems biblically accurate but not as harsh and judgmental as 'everlasting conscious punishment that will not end.'"

"Sounds good, Abner. We wouldn't want to offend anyone, you know."

That's not exactly the track Jesus took. He talked a lot about hell—more than anyone else in the Bible did. And he never once questioned if it existed or how a good God could allow people to end up there. In fact, he made it clear that he believed that after we die we'll all have to answer for our choices in life. And he didn't make it sound like the place down below would be a very nice spot for a family vacation. At the very least, Jesus's teachings portray a final justice for those who haven't accepted their reprieve.

Personally, I believe that his version of hell fits in with my picture of a loving God. After all, if there is to be final justice, there must be a hell, and if there is to be victorious love, there must be a heaven. The universe could perhaps have neither, but it couldn't have one without the other. Justice and mercy are the cornerstones of the galaxy. Heaven is proof of hell. Hell is proof of heaven. Jesus is proof of both.

Whatever your view of hell is, go to Jesus and check out what he said about it. Read his words for yourself, and then form your own view. A teaching this important shouldn't be left up to public opinion polls or something as fragile as human logic because, in the words of poet William Stafford, "following the wrong god home we may miss our star."[1]

Don't miss your star. Don't miss your home. Take Jesus at his word and find the forgiveness he offers and the assurance of love that he brings. Remember, he didn't come to condemn anyone but to save the world (see John 3:17). Listen to him whisper his "yes" to you.

Then give him your reply. Not out of fear of hell but out of thanks for heaven.

Because whenever a yes is spoken from both sides of eternity, God erases our permanent record. Permanently. And he replaces our guilt with his unconquerable love.

nineteen

lost in space

Living out the Christian life often leaves me confused. I'm not always sure how to show compassion. For example, I don't really know how to act toward homeless people. I want to treat them like Jesus would, but I don't always know what that would look like. Sometimes I give them a little change or a couple of bucks. Mostly I just walk past and pretend I don't see them. But of course I do see them, and they know that.

I'm not even sure what Jesus would do. Sometimes I think he would take them out for lunch, listen to them tell their stories, and then cruise over to Target and buy them a brand-new Made in America wardrobe. Other times I think he'd shake his head and kick 'em in the butt and say, "What's wrong with you, anyway? Get up, get a job, and stop panhandling people! If you're not willing to work, you don't deserve to eat!"

Okay, so maybe that last one isn't how Jesus would talk to them, but then again, you never know. God can be pretty blunt with freeloaders.

Many street people are drug addicts. I know that. Others are running scams. I know that too. Some aren't homeless at all; they just act like it. They panhandle all day and then drive back home to their houses in the suburbs at night. They make a killing off people's compassion.

So maybe we shouldn't give them anything. After all, we might be fueling their addictions or feeding their laziness, or they might just be taking advantage of us. That's what I tell myself sometimes when I'm walking past them, but then I have to ask, "What does that even mean—being taken advantage of?"

God doesn't seem too worried about being taken advantage of.

People take advantage of him all day long by wasting the gifts, time, life, money, moments, resources, talents, and imagination he gives us, yet he still continues to pour out his blessings on us all, even the freeloaders, even the addicts, even his enemies. He sends sunshine and summer rain to us all, not just to those who go to church or give to the United Way or hold down a steady job. As Jesus put it, "He gives his sunlight to both the evil and the good, and he sends rain on the just and on the unjust, too" (Matthew 5:45).

And besides, if we really believe that everything we have comes from God, then we're not the ones being taken advantage of if we give our stuff away—God is. And still he tells us to do it. As Jesus told his followers, "Freely you have received, freely give" (Matthew 10:8 NIV).

It's a little disconcerting to me that Jesus never warned against being taken advantage of. He never said, "Give to those who ask you—if you trust them." He never cautioned against giving to people who might not make wise choices with the gift: "Give to those who ask you—unless they look like they're gonna use it to buy booze or something." He never warned us about lending to someone who might not be able to repay us.

Instead he said, "Give what you have to anyone who asks you for it; and when things are taken away from you, don't try to get them back. . . . Love your enemies! Do good to them! Lend to them! And don't be concerned that they might not repay" (Luke 6:30, 35). This makes it sound like we should *expect* to be taken advantage of, not be wary of it. He even ties this type of life in with heavenly rewards: "Then your reward from heaven will be very great, and you will truly be acting as children of the

Most High, for he is kind to the unthankful and to those who are wicked. You must be compassionate, just as your Father is compassionate" (Luke 6:35–36). Once Jesus even told people to be careful *not* to do things for people who would be able to pay them back (see Luke 14:12–14).

When my friend Mark first pointed these verses out to me, I asked the obvious question, "Okay then, what if someone asks you for your house? Would you give it to him—and if you would, can I have yours?"

But almost before he could answer, I realized what I was doing. I was trying to make following Jesus look ludicrous. I was really saying, "Let's not get carried away here, Mark. Let's not take this following Jesus thing too far. It's not sensible to live like that. Jesus couldn't possibly have meant what he said."

But what if he did?

∾

Lots of times I just drive past hitchhikers and stalled motorists, thinking that someone else will stop, or that they should just use their cell phone and call for help, or that I have more important things to do anyway, but then once in a while I'll remember Jesus's story of the man from Samaria who showed mercy (see Luke 10:25–37). "Now, go and do likewise," Jesus said. So sometimes I do stop.

One time I picked up a homeless guy in Georgia who was hitchhiking back to his hometown in Tennessee to see his daughter, or at least that's the line he used with me.

During our ride he told me what it's like to live on the road. He explained that if you look behind a grocery store on the edge of most medium-sized towns, you'll find a woods where homeless people go to live in hobo condos (his term, not mine). "There's dumpsters back there, and you can get cardboard and food too," he said. "You'd be amazed what people throw away."

Later, when I got home, I kept my eyes open and asked around and found out that in our town, that place is White's Grocery Store over by the railroad tracks at the base of Buffalo Mountain.

Once when I left the video store in the strip mall across the street from White's, I saw a homeless man standing with his dog beneath the overhanging roof of the video place. They were watching a storm pummel the parking lot with rain.

"Some storm, huh?" I said.

He nodded without looking at me. The air around him smelled like old sweat and stale beer and damp pavement.

"Do you live behind White's Grocery Store?" I asked him.

He looked at me curiously, sizing me up. Maybe he was wondering if I was a cop and he was in trouble. "Yeah," he said at last. I didn't know what else to say. I stood there nodding for a minute or two and then said, "See ya," and I left him there watching the storm with his dog as I jogged through the rain to my car so I could go home and watch my movies.

After traveling for about an hour with the guy who told me about the hobo condos, he had to use the bathroom. So I pulled into a Hardee's restaurant, and while we were there, I offered to buy him a cheeseburger.

"No thanks," he said.

"But you have to eat something. C'mon, I'll buy it for you and then you can have it later, when you're more hungry."

Then he smiled wide, his way of showing me that he didn't have any teeth. He didn't want a cheeseburger because he couldn't eat a cheeseburger. So I bought one cheeseburger (for me) and two cups of coffee, and we filed back into my car. I wondered aloud what he actually did eat. "Soup," he told me.

He showed me his belongings then. He carried everything he owned in a Ziploc sandwich bag. Here's a list of his worldly possessions: a toothbrush, a well-worn pocket-sized New Testament, a small bar of gritty-looking soap, a nubby little pencil, a voter registration card with an address he used to have, and a well-weathered picture of his daughter, taken five years earlier. "I hope to see her again someday," he said.

He told me that in the homeless community, there's a lot of stealing from other homeless people. Lots of crime. "It's better not to have a lot of stuff."

"I see."

"You can find 'most everything you need along the highway. Clothes. Shoes. I found this shirt." He pointed to the one he was wearing.

"Oh. I see."

Since then, whenever I walk along the highway, I always keep an eye out for stuff, and I discovered the guy was right. Next to the dead possums and blown-out tires, you can find all sorts of handy things. I found a shovel one time, and a set of car keys, and a bungee cord, and even a washing machine. I saw clothes there too. I kept the bungee cord and the shovel. I left the clothes and the car keys and the washing machine for someone else.

One summer when I was in Denver, riding the airport shuttle to a hotel, I saw a Hispanic man sitting by a stop sign, staring straight ahead, holding up a dingy piece of cardboard on which he'd written this:

Spaceship Broken.
Need Parts.
God bless you. Peace and love.

The shuttle driver signaled and turned left before that homeless man, lost in the universe, could make eye contact with me. I wonder how he felt being so far from home, with no way to get back to the place he belonged.

◈

Not all hitchhikers are homeless, but many of the ones I've met are. When I pick them up, they ask me if it's okay if they smoke in my car. None have ever lit up without politely asking first. I don't smoke and find it hard to breathe around people who do, but I always lie and tell them I don't mind. I think they can tell I'm lying, because they roll down the window before lighting up.

Usually they're quiet and respectful, calling me "sir" and thanking me repeatedly for giving them a lift. Sometimes they ask me to forgive them if they don't smell right. Sometimes they tell me their stories. Most of the time they ask me for money. Some of them are drunk or high.

I often wonder what Billy Graham would say to a homeless person on a drive through the country. I'm sure he'd take the time to share the gospel with them and to pray for them. I like to tell the gospel story myself, but I often find that trying to do it with strangers in my car creates an awkwardness, and the distance between the driver's seat and the passenger seat grows bigger until we can barely hear each other anymore. Then the person I'm with remembers he needs to be let out at the next exit, and that's that.

However, I do want people to know the story of Jesus, to experience it for themselves, so sometimes I do witness to homeless people. But then, while I'm telling them how much God loves them and has a plan for their life, I wonder what I'd be thinking if I were in their place: *Well, if he loves me so much, how come I'm like this? How come I don't have any food? How come I'm a drunk? How come I don't have a home?* I'm glad they're respectful enough not to ask me those questions, because I'm not sure I know the answers.

Sometimes when I see people on the corner of University Parkway and South Roan Street (the nearest intersection to White's Grocery Store), I ask them to come over to our house. I invited a guy over a few years ago when I was building a tree house for my kids. As he climbed into the passenger seat of my car, he told me his name was Gary. "You can smoke if you want to," I said. He rolled down the window and lit his cigarette.

When we arrived at my house, my three daughters stared wide-eyed at him and loved him right away.

"Gary doesn't have a house to live in," I told Eden, who was four at the time.

"Oh," she said thoughtfully, probably trying to picture what that would be like. Then she said, "He can live here with us." She's a little girl. She doesn't understand these things.

Gary and I went outside to work on the tree house, but I was afraid he would fall from the planks I'd positioned up in the tree, so I gave him some leftover two-by-fours and asked him to work on a small bridge over a place in the woods where a stream used to be.

"I'm good with a hammer," said Gary.

"Great," I said.

Gary was bad with a hammer. He never did finish the bridge. He mostly just sat there catching his breath since his emphysema was so bad, telling my kids stories about the Vietnam War. Later, after he left, I had to redo all the work he did on the bridge and explain to my daughters what Napalm was.

Liesl made us soup and coffee, and after about an hour, Gary told me he had to get going. We gave him some chocolate pudding in a disposable plastic cup, a plastic spoon, and five dollars cash. He asked me to drop him off at the street corner near White's so he could catch the bus to the shelter for supper. So that's where I left him. As I drove off he thanked me, coughed, and lit up a cigarette.

When I got back home, Eden asked where Gary was. She'd been cleaning her room so he could stay there.

She's a little girl. She doesn't understand these things.

∾

One snowy day in January I picked up a guy on that street corner near White's. I don't even remember his name anymore. I wanted to help him, but had forgotten my wallet at home, so I invited him to hop in the car with me, and he did. The farther we drove into the country toward my home, the more nervous he became. He was obviously drunk and only somewhat aware of what was going on. "You ain't gonna take me off somewhere and murder me, are ya?" he asked me at last.

"No," I said, thinking it was a little strange that he was the one scared of me. "I just need to get my credit card."

I asked Liesl to warm up some soup, and I called the Comfort Inn, the closest hotel to White's Grocery Store, but they were full. The Days Inn, about a mile away, had one room left.

I gave him a sleeping bag that I don't really think he wanted because it would be too hard for him to carry around or it would get stolen, but I didn't know what else to do, what with it snowing outside and all. I gave him a stocking cap too. Then I drove him to the Days Inn.

I dropped him off at his room. "You can tell your friends you spent the night at a hotel," I said piously. But he didn't seem too impressed. "I hope my stuff is okay in the woods," he told me. "I hope no one steals it. And how'm I supposed to get back?"

"Um, I guess you'll have to walk."

Then, without another word, he closed the door. I wonder if he carries around pictures of his family in a plastic bag. I wonder what his name was.

I wonder where he slept the next night.

I have a sheet metal shed on the edge of the woods behind my house. We keep our lawn mower there, the blow-up kiddie pool, the girls' bikes, things like that. Oil stains cover the floor. It smells like gasoline in there. And one day I actually caught myself thinking, *Maybe the homeless guys could stay there, or in my garage.*

I don't typically think, *Maybe I could sleep on the floor of my garage or move into the shed for a few weeks and give this guy my bedroom.* I don't think things like that. I'm too mature. But my four-year-old daughter cleaned her room so Gary could stay there.

I don't know what to do when I meet people like that man in the snow. Before I met Jesus, I would have just driven past. Life wasn't so confusing back then.

∾

The most memorable guy was Don. I saw him holding a sign that said, "WILL WORK FOR FOOD." I'd just printed up some brochures, so I asked him to come over to my apartment and help me fold them.

"That's it?" he said.

"Yeah."

"Sounds easy."

It was easy, but Don was about as good at folding brochures as Gary was at nailing two-by-fours. As he systematically ruined my stack of newly printed brochures, Don told us about his wife, who lived three and a half hours away in Greenville, South Carolina. As we ate soup and grilled cheese sandwiches, he said he'd needed to come to our town for medical help at the VA hospital and that she was back home alone.

"I don't know how to get back to see her," he said, eyeing me.

"I could drive you," I said stupidly, without thinking. I was able to tell how stupid it was after only one glance at my wife's face.

"Oh, no," said Don with a wave of his hand. "I couldn't ask you to do that. But," he added, staring into the corner of the room, "I could use some money for a bus ticket."

Liesl and I talked it over and agreed to buy him a bus ticket to Greenville, South Carolina. After finding out the bus schedule, I dropped him off at the bus depot a few minutes before the bus was scheduled to leave.

"God bless you," he said.

"God bless you too."

And then he walked over and got on the bus. I didn't wait around to see if he was on the bus when it left. I figured he might not be, and I didn't want to see him sneak off. I wanted his story to be true.

That's the night Liesl and I were robbed.

At 4:03 a.m. she shook me awake. "Did you hear something?"

"No," I mumbled, but the truth was, yes, I was hearing something. I thought it was in my dreams.

"Wake up!" she said, shaking me again.

I moaned. The sounds came again. Breaking glass.

I sat up. By then my heart was jackhammering in my chest. "Um, okay. I heard that." You tend to wake up rather quickly when you hear someone smashing one of the windows to your apartment.

"Do something!" she squealed.

"What?" I know it sounds stupid and cowardly, but I had no idea what to do. My father had never given me lessons on how a man should respond when he's being burgled, and macho doesn't come natural to most of us. We need role models for that sort of thing. That's why we watch James Bond flicks and read Tom Clancy novels.

I don't own a gun, and I didn't keep a baseball bat under my pillow. I guess I could have maybe kicked him around with some karate moves, but the closest I'd ever come to studying karate was watching Jet Li movies.

I glanced around, scanning the room for something I could use to protect my family. Lying in the doorway to our bedroom was one of the girls' naked Barbie dolls.

For a moment I wondered what kind of damage Jet Li could do with a naked Barbie doll. It would probably be fatal. Barbie's feet are pretty hard and pointy, come to think of it. I could perhaps use her like a knife and fend off the robber by stabbing him with Barbie's pointy little feet. "Someone is climbing in the window!" Liesl gasped, interrupting my Barbie foot defense plans.

I peered out the bedroom window. Sure enough, a man was crawling into our kitchen window. I decided against using Barbie to defend my home and hurried toward the hallway.

The nearest phone was beyond the kitchen in the living room, so I'd need to get past the burglar just to call the police. I shuffled down the hall in my boxer shorts, trying to look menacing. I don't believe I was very successful.

When I was halfway down the hallway, the sounds in the kitchen stopped. That meant the burglar either was inside the apartment or had fled outside. I gulped and, still unsure what to do, edged closer to the kitchen. When I finally peered around the corner, no one was there. The window was shattered, the screen was torn, and an iron and a bottle of dishwashing soap were missing. I checked all throughout our apartment to make sure we were safe. Empty. The robber had fled.

"Is there anyone there?" called Liesl.

"He's gone," I said. "Took your iron."

"What? My iron?"

"I guess it was the only thing within reach next to the window." I glanced down at my plaid boxer shorts. "I guess I scared him off."

I put on some clothes and called the police then, even though I didn't really expect them to find our iron being fenced on the black market somewhere.

"I can't guarantee anything," said the very serious-looking officer. "Do you have any idea who it might have been?"

"Um, no. I don't know."

"Did you see anyone strange around here earlier today?"

I decided it was probably a good thing he hadn't seen me coming down the hallway in my underwear making my menacing face.

"Well?"

"Um, no." Only then did I look up and see our money jar on top of the refrigerator and remember inviting Don over to fold brochures. Of course Don had seen our money up there because that's where I'd gotten the cash to pay for his bus ticket to South Carolina so that he could return to his wife. Thankfully, I could see it was still full. "No," I told the officer at last. "No one strange."

That's why Don is the most memorable one, even though I still don't know if it was him that night—if he's the man who ripped a hole through our screen, smashed the window, crawled into my apartment at 4:03 a.m., and stole an iron and a bottle of dishwashing liquid.

I never saw him again.

The police never found the iron.

"WILL WORK FOR FOOD," his sign had said.

I wonder if he ever made it back to see his wife.

It would be easy to keep walking by and pretending we don't see them, or to close up our lives even tighter so we don't get taken advantage of. I do it all too often. But then I remember that Jesus left Judas in charge of the money for his group even though Judas was a thief. Apparently Jesus wasn't too concerned with being taken advantage of. He was more concerned about other things.

I once spoke at a church during a special youth night and told the story about Don. They were studying 1 John 3:17–18: "If anyone has material possessions and sees his brother in need but has no pity on him, how can the love of God be in him? Dear children, let us not love with words or tongue but with actions and in truth" (NIV). I asked them what we should do when we see people in need and we have the possessions to help them. I asked them how we can even call ourselves believers if we turn our backs on someone in need. I asked them if the starving orphaned children in Africa count as brothers in need. They listened to me politely.

I asked them all those things because I needed someone to ask them of me, and no one ever had. I remembered reading somewhere that St.

Francis of Assisi had said, "Is it not a form of stealing to keep something for yourself when you meet someone who needs it more?" I asked them what they thought of that. They listened quietly. Someone in the back of the room coughed.

The teens were staying in the church that night, sleeping in cardboard boxes in order to experience what it's really like to live on the streets. (They didn't go to a park or an underpass for safety reasons.) The church had central air. There were snack machines in the lobby. But the students did have to wear old clothes, so there was that.

When I was done, I pointed to the pile of leftover clothes from the Goodwill store in the corner of the room. "What's gonna happen to those?" I asked.

"They're gonna shred 'em tomorrow," my youth pastor friend told me.

"Really?" I said. An expensive down coat lay on the top of the stack. "Hey, that one's pretty nice."

"You can have it," he told me, picking it up, "if you give it to a homeless person." Well, at least he'd been listening to my message.

"Okay, I will." I felt very righteous and spiritual taking that coat. I could almost hear harp music in the background. I tried hard to forget that only a moment earlier I'd been wondering if the coat might fit me.

So I left the church and headed downtown to give the coat away to a homeless man. It was the middle of the night in late November. I drove up and down the streets looking for cold, coatless, homeless street people. It didn't take me long to realize that I didn't have any idea where homeless people in my town sleep. Of course, now I know they sleep behind White's Grocery Store, but at the time I didn't have a clue where to look. I tried the downtown streets; I drove under the bridges and past the public housing areas. After half an hour I gave up and headed home with the coat still in my car.

The next day I had to go to Chicago with my family, so I brought the coat along. I asked the pastor at the church we were visiting if they had anyone there who could use a new coat.

"Oh, yes," she said.

"Would you give this to 'em?" I handed her the down coat from the Goodwill store in Tennessee. She nodded her thanks.

I felt better then—I know, I know, I didn't *technically* give the coat to a homeless person, but at least I'd done my part. The problem wasn't mine anymore. Which was good because the longer I'd held on to that coat, the worse I'd begun to feel. Having it in my possession made me uncomfortable.

When I was in Atlanta last summer, standing on a street corner waiting for the walk signal, I asked my friend Doc what we should do about homeless people, what the solution was.

"Do what Giuliani did. He cleaned up New York City," Doc told me.

"How?"

"Got rid of 'em. Sent some of 'em to the hospitals."

"Oh. That's good," I said. "What about the rest?"

"The rest he sent somewhere else," said Doc.

"Where?"

Doc thought for a moment. "I don't know."

"But that doesn't solve the problem," I said. "Does it?"

Then the light turned green, and we walked across the street toward our hotel.

"No, it doesn't," said Doc.

I counted the number of coats in my closet today. I own nine, most of which I never wear.

Here's something I find a bit surprising: Jesus's compassion occasionally got in the way of his ministry. In the first chapter of Mark, we find

Jesus healing everyone who was brought to him. This goes on through the night. Early the next morning, Jesus takes some time out to pray and then tells his disciples they need to move on because he had come to preach in Galilee as well.

But in the very next paragraph, yet another diseased man approaches Jesus. And Jesus, "filled with compassion," heals him (Mark 1:41 NIV). As a result of this incident, Jesus couldn't even travel openly anymore because of the mob of people that surrounded him (see Mark 1:45). Jesus healed that man even though it disrupted the efficiency of his ministry. Why?

Because he was filled with compassion. To Jesus, people were more important than ministry agendas. His compassion actually got in the way of his God-given mission, but he healed the man anyway, and God never held it against him.

I've tried to understand compassion with logic, but I can't.

Jesus didn't heal all the sick people in the world. He didn't raise all the dead people back to life. And even those he did heal became sick again. Those he raised to life all died again. So what was the point? What did it ultimately matter? What difference did it make?

It made a difference at that time, in that place, to that person. And that was enough.

That's the logic of love. Compassion says, "You can't decipher how the world will unfold. You can't weigh love in a scale and determine the course of the greatest good and the least suffering. And so, at this time, in this place, in this way, show compassion to this person. By doing that you will fulfill the law of love, which is impractical, illogical, unpredictable, unreasonable, and at the same time the greatest thing you can do with your life."

Then the King will turn to those on the left and say, "Away with you, you cursed ones, into the eternal fire prepared for the Devil and his demons! For I was hungry, and you didn't feed me. I was thirsty, and you didn't give me anything to drink. I was a stranger, and you didn't invite me into your home. I was naked, and you gave me no clothing. I was sick and in prison, and you didn't visit me."

Then they will reply, "Lord, when did we ever see you hungry or thirsty or a stranger or naked or sick or in prison, and not help you?" And he will answer, "I assure you, when you refused to help the least of these my brothers and sisters, you were refusing to help me."

Matthew 25:41–45

Sometimes the king is seated on his throne in heaven, ruling the universe with his nail-scarred hands. Sometimes he carries his life in a Ziploc bag. And sometimes he's sitting by a street corner with a sign that says, "Spaceship Broken. Need Parts. God bless you. Peace and love."

I heard that one day a journalist asked Mother Teresa, "When you see how many people are hurting, how can you ever expect to be successful?"

And she replied, "God hasn't asked me to be successful." Then she walked over to help a dying man.

I think I know his name.

through the birth canal

In comic books and fairy tales, death is never the end of the story, because the toxic waste that the superhero fell into actually acts as an antidote to phosophonic ray guns (*of course! How could we forget that?*) and the tears of the grieving princess landing on the cheek of the dead prince awaken him because her love is stronger than even the witch's wicked, thorn-encrusted spell.

You can always bring someone back from the dead in a myth, but in real life, children really do drown in bathtubs while their babysitters talk on the phone in the living room, and despite their parents' screams and tears and trembling love, nothing can bring them back. Funerals really do interrupt our lives, bringing everything else to a screeching, heart-rending, terrifying halt.

> one day we found a dead bunny in the yard. it wasn't fun to play with and we couldn't leave it there or it would attract the wrong kind of flies.
> so we buried it beneath a spreading tree and said a prayer and my daughters watched their first dead body get lowered into the ground

on a sunny day when all we wanted to do was hang up the laundry and play tag in the tall, leaning grass.

∽

Fairy tale endings are for fairy tales. We know that, because real life is filled with strokes and morgues and unanswered prayers and broken dreams. And broken hearts. Grief and regret stain the cover pages of our souls. So we tell ourselves these stories of happily ever after and once upon a time. But we all know it would be too much to ask for a story like that to actually come true.

Yet in the midst of it all comes a whisper of another world, another reality, echoing through the centuries. *Easter*. A truth beyond truths. *Easter*. A tune strong enough to overpower any funeral dirge. *Easter*. Here is a tale that stretches beyond eternity. Here is a love the tomb cannot contain.

"You will grieve," said the Storyteller of the Ages, "but your grief will turn to joy" (John 16:20 NIV). Like a mother who forgets the pains of childbirth the moment she looks into the eyes of her newborn, joy can come crashing in and wash the ache of this world away. Here is a wall of joy that is stronger than the world's deepest grief.

I think Jesus's words to his disciples are just as true for us as they were for them. "A woman giving birth to a child has pain," he said, "because her time has come; but when her baby is born she forgets the anguish because of her joy that a child is born into the world. So with you: Now is your time of grief, but I will see you again and you will rejoice, and no one will take away your joy" (John 16:21–22 NIV).

Now is our time of anguish. Here on this inexplicable planet of ulcers and fear and graveyards and grief. As we bury our loved ones and bury our guilt and try not to yell so much at the kids. As we glimpse death grinning on the edge of the night, mouthing our name. According to St. Paul, our entire world is groaning as in the pains of childbirth (see

Romans 8:22). But the message of Easter is that the final chorus of the galaxy is joy, not pain. The final refrain is life after death to all who believe. Even now, hope is real because Easter is real, and because of that we'll really see Jesus again and receive a joy that no one, that nothing, will be able to take away.

The journey through life's questions and pain and unanswered prayers leads me past the crux to the empty tomb, brings me to the risen Savior.

In a stunningly real way, the empty tomb is God's poem for our planet, with stanzas drenched in blood and dreams. The notes of this song ring with the cries of a newborn child in a dingy stable . . . the sound of a whip against a carpenter's back . . . the hearty laughter of a groom carrying his bride across the threshold on their wedding night. From Eden to eternity, from a choice in a garden to a man on a cross, from a straw-filled manger to an empty grave—here is the fairy tale that is finally true.

And it is not a neat and tidy tale with clean, uncrinkled pages. This is a bloodstained story, dirtied with tears and ripe with both pain and glory. It is not a nice moral lesson; it is sometimes a scream in the still of the night, sometimes a teardrop at the break of dawn.

Easter is a promise bigger than life itself: a God dying for those who kill him. It is the ultimate paradox of love, offering a doorway to the greatest once upon a time of all.

༄

Honestly, I have a tough time when I'm asked to speak at a church on Easter weekend because there isn't anything in real life to compare this to, this rising from the dead. Caterpillars and butterflies, yes, yes, I know. But we all know it's not the same thing. Nothing is.

So our explanations of that day often end up sounding like a tale either too good to be true or too unbelievable to be taken seriously. Because of that, I sometimes hear pastors telling their congregations how they're *supposed* to feel at Easter—full of joy and hope and peace and so on. But manufactured emotions don't last. So we shake his hand and thank him for the sermon and head home to eat sliced ham and potato salad, and pretty soon life on this fractured planet gets right back to normal again. We're back in the middle of our troubled marriages and our battles with breast cancer and our cell phone bills and our quiet little addictions. But nothing much has changed.

Here's what I've learned over the years: before I can really capture the true fragrance of Easter, I have to see myself in the tale. And that means not only the awkward admission of my own mortality but also the true confession of my own sins.

We all have shady groves in our hearts and terrifyingly stormy skies raging in our souls. Good and bad intertwine within us. Life is not all light and lilies; it is heartache and pain and a naked Messiah dying on Calvary's cross.

The springtime of Easter only follows the cold clutch of winter. So before we can really experience the joy that no one can take away, we need to walk up the dark and mysterious road to the cross where we acknowledge the deep grief of death and loss, the shame of our unbelief and sin, and the part we played in the death of our Savior.

Of course, this isn't fun or comfortable, so most of the time we don't do it. We try to leap over the tentacles of grief and land in the arms of joy, to get from Good Friday to Easter Sunday without having to experience the mourning of that dark, hope-drained Saturday. But when I look deeply into my heart, I see venom pulsing through my past—pain I've caused by the choices I've made, friends I've hurt by the words I've said. These are the reasons for the scars on his hands.

And his love is the reason for the empty tomb.

For then, on Sunday morning, the tale turns. We flip the page and find that the hero is alive. A new story is whispered through time. *Life. Love. Peace.*

sailing between the stars

Death has no more sting.

The tale of joy has won.

The sail has been raised to catch the breeze that's blowing across the wild, starry waves.

It's no mere coincidence that conversion is explained in Scripture as the death of the self. To come to Jesus, we need to leave our selves behind. As Kierkegaard wrote, "Christianity teaches that you must die. Your power must be dismantled. And the life-giving Spirit is the very one who slays you. The first thing this Spirit says is that you must enter into death, you must die to yourself."[1]

People don't rejoice at Easter unless they've been through the grave themselves.

> *am i willing to die this life-giving death?*
> *this first death that conquers the last?*
> *am i willing to enter the arms of love*
> *that finally dismantle my past?*
>
> you know where the fountain of youth is,
>   you say?
> you know where dreams of
> forever can be swallowed
> in gulp after glorious gulp?
> then show me! i'll follow you anywhere!
>   yes, yes, let's go!
>
> oh, i have to die first,
>   you say?
> only then can i drink of these waters?
> well then, maybe i'll take my chances
> out here on my own, drinking from the
> sensible rivers that do not
> make such unreasonable demands.

I heard a story about a dancer who danced an incredible program. After she finished, one of the women from the audience approached her. "That was an amazing dance!" she said. "I was moved to tears, but I just have one question—what did it mean?" And the dancer replied, "If I could *tell* you what it meant, I wouldn't have had to dance it."

If Jesus could have simply told us of God's love, he wouldn't have had to dance it. If he could have explained hope after death or joy after life, he wouldn't have had to face the cross. "If there's any other way," he begged his Father in the Garden of Gethsemane, "let this cup pass from me!" (see Matthew 26:39). But there wasn't any other way. He had to walk through the grave if he was to ever take his bride's hand and invite her onto the dance floor of forever.

Take a moment right now. See the story unfold. Picture that dewy dawn. Let Easter's magic sweep through you. Hear the birds awaken the day. Feel the somber steps of the women as they head to the corpse of their God. And then, see the stone rolled away. Hear the words of the angels and feel joy erupting within you—a confused joy, an uncertain joy, a joy wrapped in question marks and exclamation points. Because if it *is* real, if he *is* alive, the text of the world has been rewritten. Death is no longer the end of the story but only a doorway toward the hearth fires of home. The fairy tale ending we thought was made up is as true as that spring breeze kissing your cheek.

Then, turn and find him within arm's reach and look into his eyes. His welcoming, wondering eyes.

Jesus offers us freshly hatched joy in his splintered, scarred hands. A joy that might get bumped and bruised on our journey across this painful planet but that can never be lost. Ever. For the risen prince has at last defeated the dragon. Death has no teeth for those who believe. In the risen Jesus we find the dreams of the world wrapped up inside skin and laughter, offering new life to all who are willing to die to themselves and enter his tale. Easter is the story of glory and pain and tears and grace that we've all been hoping would finally come true.

Step into the story again. Leap wildly in his love. Here, in his victory over death, tired souls are offered the thrilling poetry of the empty tomb and the final language of risen life. Here we find a joy that nothing, not even death, can conquer—and the timeless chorus of the breathtaking story God is telling our planet.

The empty tomb is the most intimate and essential mystery of all. It's the sailboat that catches the gusts of heaven's breath and takes us beyond the farthest reaches of the shining sea of stars.

you are the notorious one
scarred by wonder and grace.
you are the glorious opening
of a flower, to drink in
the day's first light.

the veil is lifted,
blueness careens through
the skies,
a new day awakens all around me.
shadows bury themselves in the sand
and the ocean shouts, "Triumph!"
to the shore.

notes

one in the company of fools

1. R. M. Hutchins, ed., "Pascal," in *Great Books of the Western World* (Chicago: University of Chicago, 1952), 243.

2. Kabir Helminski, ed., *The Rumi Collection* (Boston: Shambhala, 2005), 18–19.

two seeing with God-shaped eyes

1. Frederick Buechner, *Telling the Truth: The Gospel as Tragedy, Comedy, and Fairy Tale* (San Francisco: HarperSanFrancisco, 1977), 89–90.

2. I wrote a drama entitled "A Tidy Little Religion" a few years ago that explored some of these same ideas. It appears in the book *More Worship Sketches 2 Perform* (Colorado Springs: Meriwether Publishing, 2002), 169–73.

three mystery is where i live

1. Peter Kreeft, ed., *Christianity for Modern Pagans: Pascal's Pensees* (San Francisco: Ignatius Press, 1993), 139.

2. Hutchins, *Great Books of the Western World*, 238.

four good things running wild

1. G. K. Chesterton, *Orthodoxy: The Romance of Faith* (New York: Image Books, 1990), 95.

five joy on the front of my pants

1. Brian Culhane, comp., *The Treasure Chest: Memorable Words of Wisdom and Inspiration* (San Francisco: HarperSanFrancisco, 1995), 136.

six ludicrous love

1. *The Way of a Pilgrim*, trans. R. M. French (New York: Quality Paperback Book Club, 1998), 129.

2. Ibid., 131.

3. François de Fénelon, *The Seeking Heart* (Jacksonville: Christian Books Publishing House, 1992), 73.

seven   fleshing out jesus

1. Kahlil Gibran, *A Treasury of Kahlil Gibran*, ed. Martin L. Wolf (Secaucus, NJ: Citadel Press, 1974), 154–55.

2. Steven James, *Believe It: Bible Basics That Won't Break Your Brain* (Cincinnati: Standard, 2003), 52–53.

3. Flannery O'Connor, *Mystery and Manners: Occasional Prose*, ed. Sally and Robert Fitzgerald (New York: Farrar, Straus & Giroux, 2000), 96.

eight   the crux

1. Søren Kierkegaard, *Provocations: Spiritual Writings of Kierkegaard*, ed. Charles E. Moore (Maryknoll, NY: Orbis, 2003), 201.

2. Siegbert W. Becker, *The Foolishness of God* (Milwaukee: Northwestern Publishing House, 1982), 232.

ten   my biggest fan

1. John R. W. Stott, *Basic Christianity* (Downers Grove, IL: InterVarsity, 1971), 43–44.

eleven   beyond the mirage

1. Annie Dillard, *For the Time Being* (New York: Vintage Books, 1999), 107.
2. Ibid., 134.

twelve   the glass isn't half anything

1. Walt Whitman, *Leaves of Grass: The First (1855) Edition* (New York: Penguin Books, 2005), 62.

2. For example, *The Bhagavad Gita* (perhaps the most revered and sacred text for Hindus) says that a wise person "has no emotion, regardless of whether something pleasant or something unpleasant has been attained. He is not pleased, nor is he dissatisfied, and in him wisdom is established." See *The Bhagavad Gita*, trans. Bibek Debroy (New Delhi, India: Penquin Books, 2005), 39.

3. Robert Bly, James Hillman, and Michael Meade, eds., *The Rag and Bone Shop of the Heart* (New York: Harper Perennial, 1993), 97.

4. Chesterton, *Orthodoxy*, 100.

thirteen   chewing on God

1. Charles Wright, *Negative Blue* (New York: Farrar, Straus & Giroux, 2000), 105.

2. I've seen this thought brought out in the writings of Pascal, Sundar Singh, C. S. Lewis, and others. It seems to have become a favorite theme of Lewis in his later writings and is currently very much in vogue among Christian apologists.

3. Augustine, *The Confessions of St. Augustine*, trans. Rex Warner (New York: New American Library), 235.

fourteen   dance of the wills

1. Quoted in J. Manning Potts, *Listening to the Saints* (Nashville: Upper Room, 1962), 31.

2. Thomas à Kempis, *The Imitation of Christ* (Grand Rapids: Zondervan, 1983), 132.

3. Michael Card, *The Promise: A Celebration of Christ's Birth* (Nashville: Sparrow Press, 1991), 37.

4. Madame Guyon, *A Short Method of Prayer and Other Writings* (Peabody, MA: Hendrickson Publishers, 2005), 53.

5. Kierkegaard, *Provocations*, 158.

6. Thomas Merton, *No Man Is an Island* (New York: Barnes and Noble Books, 1955), xvii.

7. A. W. Tozer, *The Pursuit of God* (Christian Publications, Inc., 1948), 11, 12, 15.

8. De Fenelon, *The Seeking Heart*, 181.

9. Thomas R. Kelly, *A Testament of Devotion* (San Francisco: HarperSanFrancisco, 1992), 25.

10. Quoted in Jill Haak Adels, comp., *The Wisdom of the Saints: An Anthology* (New York: Oxford University Press, 1987), 42.

11. Brennan Manning, *The Ragamuffin Gospel* (Sisters, OR: Multnomah, 2000), 132.

12. If you're interested in unpacking more of the meaning in Jesus's stories in Luke 15, check out *Finding the Lost: Cultural Keys to Luke 15* by Kenneth E. Bailey.

13. Dag Hammarskjöld, *Markings* (New York: Alfred A. Knopf, 1991), 189.

fifteen   the monk, the chainsaw, and the king tut life-sized sarcophagus cabinet

1. Kelly, *A Testament of Devotion*, 19–20.

seventeen   the bruise on the skin of the world

1. Battistina Capalbo, ed., *Praying with Saint Teresa* (Grand Rapids: Eerdmans, 1986), 44.

2. Peter Kreeft, *Making Sense of Suffering* (Ann Arbor, MI: Servant, 1986), 22–23.

3. Okay, every time I read this paragraph, I'm struck by how logical it is, and I think, *I couldn't possibly have come up with that.* As I was researching this book I found these thoughts in my journal, and I have searched through the writings of Pascal, Kreeft, Singh, and others whom you find quoted throughout this book but can't find anyone who clarified things in this exact way, so I have to assume that it is possible I actually wrote it. With that in mind, if I did not, I give credit to whoever came up with this summary. Please don't sue me. I wanted to credit you but just couldn't figure out how.

eighteen   innocent by association

1. Bly, Hillman, and Meade, eds., *The Rag and Bone Shop of the Heart*, 233.

twenty   through the birth canal

1. Kierkegaard, *Provocations*, 149.

Steven James is an author, storyteller, and poet. He speaks weekly at conferences, churches, and special events across the country, sharing his eclectic blend of drama, comedy, and inspirational storytelling. When he's not traveling or writing, Steven likes going rock climbing, watching science fiction movies, and eating chicken fajitas. He lives with his wife and three daughters in Tennessee.

Enter the tale. Recapture the mystery.

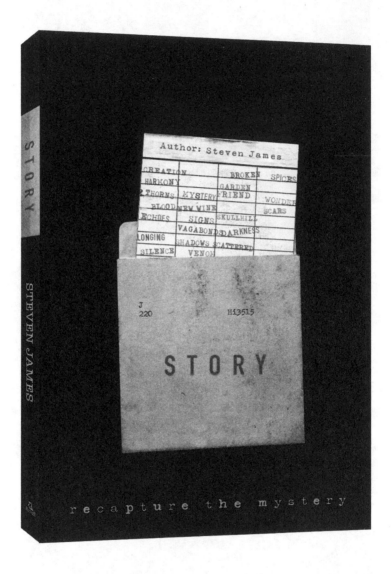

"A journey full of wonder, tears, joy, despair, and hope
revealed through the eyes and heart of a storyteller."
—*Publishers Weekly*, starred review